MW00800627

LEARNING FOR THE FUTURE

Rethinking Schools for the 21st Century

LEARNING
FOR THE
FUTURE

Rethinking Schools for the 21st Century

Gabriel Rshaid

with a contribution by
Ainsley Rose

LEAD+
LEARN
PRESS

ENGLEWOOD, COLORADO

The Leadership and Learning Center
317 Inverness Way South, Suite 150
Englewood, Colorado 80112
Phone 1.866.399.6019 I Fax 303.504.9417
www.LeadandLearn.com

Copyright © 2011 The Leadership and Learning Center
All rights reserved.

Published by Lead + Learn Press, a division of Advanced Learning Centers, Inc.

Note: Every attempt was made to obtain permission for reprint/use of contributors' work. No part of this publication may be reproduced, stored in a retrieval system, or transmitted in any form or by any means, electronic, mechanical, photocopying, recording, scanning, or otherwise, except as permitted by law, without the prior written permission of the publisher.

Limited Reproduction Permission: Permission is hereby granted to the purchaser of this book to reproduce the forms for educational and noncommercial use only.

Notice of Liability: The information in this book is distributed on an "as is" basis, without warranty. While every precaution has been taken in the preparation of the book, neither the authors nor Advanced Learning Centers, Inc., shall have any liability to any person or entity with respect to any loss or damage caused or alleged to be caused directly or indirectly by the instructions contained in this book.

All Web links in this book are correct as of the publication date but may have become inactive or otherwise modified since that time. If you notice a deactivated or changed link, please notify the publisher and specify the Web link, the book title, and the page number on which the link appears so that corrections may be made in future editions.

Lead + Learn Press also publishes books in a variety of electronic formats. Some content that appears in print may not be available in electronic books.

Library of Congress Cataloging-in-Publication Data

Rshaid, Gabriel.
  Learning for the future : rethinking schools for the 21st century / Gabriel Rshaid
with a contribution by Ainsley Rose.
      p. cm.
  Includes bibliographical references and index.
  ISBN 978-1-935588-10-8 (alk. paper)
  1. Education. 2. Teaching. I. Rose, Ainsley B., 1947- II. Title.
  LB1025.3.R75 2011
  370—dc23

                                                            2011025115

ISBN 978-1-935588-10-8
Printed in the United States of America

15 14 13 12 11   01 02 03 04 05 06 07

DEDICATION

To Ines, Belu, and Juampi,
for the many hours that this project took from them,
which they endured with
unconditional love and wisdom
that goes far beyond their years.

Contents

About the Author

 Gabriel Rshaid has been an educator for more than 20 years, having taught various subjects at the elementary and high school levels. For the last 12 years, he has been a K–12 principal in independent schools, while still remaining active in the classroom.

His passions for learning and for technological developments have taken him on the intellectual journey of thinking about education in the context of how technological changes can improve the learning process, which has led him to present in numerous venues on the topics of 21st-century education and the future of learning.

He currently resides in Buenos Aires, Argentina, with his wife and two sons.

Acknowledgments

I would like to thank Doug Reeves, who, through his vision and incredible generosity, led me along this path; Connie Kamm and Ainsley Rose, friends and mentors who are always patient and kind enough to lend an ear; Kristin Anderson, who believed in this project from the very onset—her support was key in getting it off the ground; Katie Schellhorn, who was the voice of reason throughout the process and without whose hard work and encouragement this book would not be possible; and, finally, on the home front, Sofia Sengenberger, the most amazing person that I have worked with in more than 20 years of being around schools.

Foreword
BY CONNIE KAMM

In *Learning for the Future: Rethinking Schools for the 21st Century*, Gabriel Rshaid challenges educators worldwide to shake themselves out of their outdated perspectives on teaching, leading, and learning. He points out that even though educators never intended to "create schools that would remain immune to the passage of time and ... operate in denial of current trends, [the] reality that needs to be faced is that schools have not kept up with the times." True to the book's title, Gabriel helps readers rethink what learning experiences in schools must be if educators intend to prepare children for this current knowledge era.

The introduction provides the overall focus—challenging educators to create a system that truly focuses on the talents residing within each learner rather than trying to model students' learning to their own likenesses. Gabriel also reminds educators that in this knowledge era, dedication to lifelong learning is imperative and the ability to collaborate is also highly prized.

During a time when educators throughout the world are struggling with ways to transform education, Gabriel's book is extremely opportune. To make a clear comparison between our current schools and schools of the future, he includes a highly engaging section titled "A Tale of Two Schools" where the old school is succinctly contrasted with the new school. For example, Gabriel states that in the old school, knowledge was meticulously compartmentalized and students were grouped by age. In addition, progress was calculated by averages and learning was almost always assessed by performance on sit-down written tests. It doesn't take long for the reader to recognize that the "old" school descriptions sound very much like our current school practices.

In the new school, Gabriel states that education is more about learning than teaching. He depicts a variety of environments being utilized where learning is ever-present and not relegated to the school building or traditional school hours. In this setting, education is customized to maximize the individual success of each student, and educators learn alongside their students.

If we are going to transform the way that we educate students in this new digital era, then people are going to need models and descriptions to guide them. *Learning for the Future: Rethinking Schools for the 21st Century* is a perfect companion on this journey. Throughout this thought-provoking book, Gabriel Rshaid shares his wisdom about changes in assessment, curriculum, instruction, and collaboration. He not only speaks with the voice of a futurist and a leader in education, but also from his vantage point as an effective classroom teacher who is successfully implementing the changes in classroom practice that he is urging others to make. Educators who read this book will forever change the way they think about teaching, leading, and learning.

Introduction

In the space of a little less than a decade—the mere blink of an eye in historical terms—the whole world of education turned upside down.

Most of us who started in the profession did so because we enjoyed teaching—because of those "aha!" moments in which we managed to transmit what we had learned to our students. Our role was indispensable in passing on our knowledge. Other than textbooks, which could not possibly cover the breadth and depth required, our pupils depended solely on our accumulated wisdom and, essentially, on our skills as teachers, to make content accessible, engaging, and understandable.

This ages-old model made a lot of sense, in that subsequent stages in the educational process built cumulatively upon the previous set of knowledge. The end result acquired, namely to gain proficiency in a more or less narrowly defined field of study, was well suited for a marketplace that required mastery of specific tasks amidst clear expectations for success.

But that isn't the case any longer. The advent and generalization of the Internet, second only (or perhaps not "second" anymore) to the invention of the printing press by Gutenberg in granting universal access to information, transformed what began as a pedagogy of poverty into one of infinite abundance. The fact that we are, indeed, the first generation in history to have full access to the whole array of accumulated human knowledge is a fine and noble challenge for humanity, but, for us mere mortals in the teaching profession, it implies a complete redefinition not only of our job descriptions, but also of our personal roles in the educational process.

Authors, pedagogues, and self-proclaimed gurus have extensively written on what are generally known as the "21st-century skills" that emerge from this new scenario. It is unquestionable that a completely new set of skills must be taught to allow our students to function effectively within this totally new environment, and that many valuable resources have been developed to help teachers bridge the gap between this present that we don't understand and a future that we cannot predict. However, despite some laudable emerging efforts by innovative educators, little has been accomplished at the classroom level and the "21st-Century Skills" phrase is at risk of becoming yet another educational cliché.

Despite the onset of the 21st century's second decade, implementation of these skills has merely scratched the surface, and momentum is sagging. Advocate groups, multimillion-dollar investments, and goodwill governmental efforts in various countries have yielded only token results, and our schools are largely what they still were in the 19th and 20th centuries.

One cannot help but wonder what went wrong, other than what is self-evident: the time lag between reality and educational reform, fast-paced changes that are disorienting and distressing, and a generation of educators who grew up and learned in a completely different world from their students, who have thought processes that are unimaginable to adults.

But there is far more than that. Our deeply ingrained obsession with safety and incremental risks have led us to try to change our educational system one small step at a time, with the ongoing result of unsuccessfully attempting to adapt an ill-fitting model to a completely new paradigm. We are essentially trying to fit a round peg into a square hole. Social scientists have long known that the open-ended nature of the 21st century, and the intrinsic complexity of the infinite knowledge scenario, do not lend themselves at all to a left-brained, sequentially planned, reward-and-punishment approach that will forever fall short of the mark in catching up with change, and that will leave behind a trail of frustration and disengagement. We might be a generation of transition, but if we educators do not change our own educational paradigm to face the new knowledge paradigm, we will not only not accomplish our goal of preparing our students for the 21st century (only nine-tenths of it is left as of now!), but we will miss out on our one and only chance to capture the public's imagination and make true on the promise of lifelong learning.

This book is not about unrealistically proposing to overhaul our schools and our whole system of education, but rather about a new mindset and a related road map to approach our mission as educators, one that focuses not only on contents, pedagogy, new skills, and a new curriculum, but that also gives importance to the personal dimension of teachers and learners, or rather to the learners that we *all* are now. If we wish to be the protagonists of a period in history in which we make good use of the vast amounts of knowledge now available to find the elusive solutions to the problems that have assailed us from the beginning of time—hunger, war, religious hatred, poverty, and other inexplicable current evils—we must develop a new collective awareness of humanity through refocusing our educational system on the person. The greatest outcome of the 21st century is not that knowledge is horizontally accessible to every child, but that every child can learn. It is our moral imperative to uncover, like Michelangelo did with *David*, the angel that lies dormant in the stone—the students' own hidden talents—and not to try to model their learning to our own likenesses.

Throughout this book, we will attempt to show that a renewed approach in our schools is possible even within the constraints under which we operate; that it technically makes sense, and therefore is our best bet for meeting head on the seemingly unfathomable challenge of 21st-century education. This different mindset can jump-start the process through which we can transform the knowledge era into better standards of living. And even more importantly, it can become a self-fulfilling process for all involved, thus allowing us to free ourselves from that overpowering threat of failure that seems to gnaw at the very essence of educational reform and that has so far inhibited us from, in the words of Neil Armstrong, turning our small steps into that giant leap that we so badly need.

CHAPTER ONE

The Challenge

THE STORY OF EDUCATION IN THE 21ST CENTURY is like that of a family who had been poor for countless generations suddenly inheriting hundreds of millions of dollars from a distant relative they did not even know existed. Because the adults in the family have such deeply ingrained habits of living in poverty, they cannot understand that they are infinitely rich, and they continue living as if nothing has changed. They are like people from a primitive civilization who are suddenly exposed to modern life in a big city—baffled by it all and clueless as to where to start.

However, the children in this family, who because of their young age have not developed the ingrained traits of living in poverty, understand far better what it means to be rich, and demand to reap the benefits of their wealth. So the parents, instead of coming to terms with this new reality and trying to learn how to dispose well of their newly acquired fortune in order to guide their young offspring, opt for giving their sons and daughters credit cards with no spending limits.

As ridiculous as this may seem, this story bears a strong resemblance to what has happened during the last few years in education.

The widespread development of the Internet and the ensuing limitless availability of online resources have dramatically changed the landscape of education in a very short time. From being constrained by our own acquired knowledge and physical access to limited sources of information (textbooks, reference books)—what, in retrospect, we can call a *pedagogy of poverty*—we have moved to one of infinite abundance, in which almost anything we wish to learn can be found just a few keystrokes away. And instead of celebrating and attempting to administer this incomparable wealth, we educators have instead chosen largely to retreat into ourselves and our outdated teaching and learning methods, whilst watching with concern how the younger generation attempts to discover the benefits of having unrestricted access to information, more often than not driven by market forces and not educationally sound advice.

THE NEW PARADIGM

In the past, the invention of the printing press spurred a phenomenon known as "disintermediation," allowing universal access to books that had been previously restricted to specific places that housed treasured manuscripts, such as monasteries or libraries. Similarly, or even much more so, the advent of the Internet and the lowering cost of broadband connections generated an unplanned development that, in the space of just a few years, revolutionized the whole concept of learning, giving birth to the *knowledge era*.

Exponential growth of online content resulted in horizontal access to information for anybody with a Web connection, destroying the old paradigm built upon the value of possessing information as a prerequisite to doing anything important in life. This completely mind-boggling new paradigm is one of infinite knowledge, and as such of limitless possibilities for learning.

Add to that the fact that the world has gone "flat"—that all conceivable barriers have been torn down (a key point that we will come back to repeatedly)—and we find ourselves amidst a perplexing new scenario. In addition to having access to unlimited knowledge, being able to effectively interact with our counterparts from all over the world in a globalized context has leveled the playing field. And like in any game, we need to find, both individually and collectively, what our role is and how we can effectively be ourselves in playing it.

In *The World is Flat* (2007), his book on how information technology has reshaped the landscape of businesses and education, Thomas Friedman refers to this changing world as ". . . a global, Web-enabled playing field that allows for multiple forms of collaboration on research and work in real time, without regard to geography, distance or, in the near future, even language."

Advances in telecommunications and the ability to share documents seamlessly across platforms enable collaboration in unprecedented ways. Today's world offers unlimited potential for effective collaboration, and gives a completely new dimension to the idea of teamwork. Individuals who are not able to function effectively as positive members of a team are finding that they are dysfunctional in today's society.

Another radical change in the paradigm has to do with languages and the way we communicate. Because of the old model based on printing, text was the one and only medium of expression, and the whole educational system was almost exclusively focused on teaching students how to decode (read and comprehend) and write. Without making any value judgment on the associated benefits to the development of children that result from an emphasis on reading and writing, the hard fact is that all of us consume much more in terms of audiovisual expression than reading, and that both in the workplace and in academia the evolving language is multimedia. Because our educational systems do not train us to decode multimedia content and read between the lines (for example, we have not even developed a lexicon to express the process of "making inferences based on multimedia sources," and so we need to resort to using the inadequate word "reading" to refer to that process), we are instantly at a disadvantage with respect to consuming the evolving media. Even though most adults are required to generate multimedia content in whatever environment we work or study in, we generally do not receive even basic training on how to do so. Suggesting a shift away from reading and writing and towards evolving media can seem educationally blasphemous, but the hard facts, which suggest that such a shift is necessary, are incontrovertible. Denial might achieve short-term comfort, but failing to address the new landscape will inevitably shortchange our students and their learning.*

* The Spring 2010 release of Ipsos OTX MediaCT's Longitudinal Media Experience (LMX) study on more than 7,000 online consumers ages 13 to 74 show that people spend more than half their waking day with media (www.ipsos-na.com).

These developments have been unplanned, and brought about mostly by market forces and the push by companies to develop technological advances based on sales and revenues rather than what would be best for humanity. So, even though these technological advances have opened up fantastic possibilities for education, the forces that drive them are not naturally tuned in to educationally sound developments. Contending with this new paradigm and attempting to make the best of it falls on the already heavily burdened shoulders of schools and educators.

THE "PROMISED LAND"

For years, we have been writing school mission statements that look at us reproachfully from their glass-mounted shrines on our school walls, extolling lifelong learning for our students in an environment that does not always succeed in providing it. But at long last, the field of education has put its own happy twist on a phrase borrowed from Canadian Prime Minister Pierre Trudeau—we are not yet at the promised land, but we can see it from here.

Deep down, we all strive to turn our students into that mythical creature, the lifelong learner. We want to seed our students with an unquenchable desire for learning that will result in them never dropping a book from their hands, and taking advantage of every available opportunity for learning. But we know that only a chosen few will be bitten by the bug and actually have the drive to continue learning throughout life. (Some of them might even become teachers!)

In the past, the main obstacle between us and this implicitly utopian goal was that learning required a physical and financial commitment on the part of the learner. Pursuing a higher education degree, seeking mentors, finding good books, surviving the occasional frustration of sterile academic research and biased or erroneous sources, and subscribing to journals and magazines all required that the learner have the motivation and the stamina to go that extra mile to pursue learning.

None of that is required now. A reasonably good Internet connection is the only physical requirement for lifelong learning. If we have the skills to find it, the knowledge is there, either to bake a cheesecake or build the home version of a nuclear reactor. Like never before, we are able to solve problems about which we know nothing, and can easily learn about any topic we might be interested in, and then keep updated and current on it.

Lifelong learning is not only possible, but a prerequisite to functioning effectively in modern life. We live in times in which the only certainty is change, a change that takes place at such breathtaking speed that we struggle to interpret trends and tendencies and, in general, to understand what is going on in the present. The future is a completely different challenge than any we have faced thus far, and it is universally acknowledged that we are preparing students for jobs that do not exist at present, and for a future that we cannot predict.

The name of the game is to "unlearn" and "relearn." We need to have a mindset such that we are not only open to learning new things all the time, but also flexible enough to forget the old ways of doing those things, because the "old ways" might be counterproductive to learning.

Maybe a poster should be visible in every classroom telling us that we are the first generation of learners to be able to delve into all accumulated human knowledge, as a reminder not only of the endless possibilities we have, but also of the huge responsibility we face in getting it right in our classrooms, so that we can translate that infinite knowledge into improved living and a greater collective awareness of humanity.

Moses and the Training Program

Ron Heifetz (2006) uses in his keynotes on leadership the Old Testament story of Moses as a good metaphor for organizational change. Moses took 20 years to lead his people to the promised land, even though it was within grasp. He had the vision, he could literally see it amidst the wanderings of his people, but he knew they were not yet ready to get there. His 20 years in the desert were nothing but a training program.

As we educators are charged with leading the younger generation to the "promised land," we are faced with the immensity of the task and the challenges awaiting us. Heifetz and coauthor Marty Linsky (2002) make a distinction between challenges that are technical (those that require specific solutions) and adaptive (those that have no single right answer but that necessitate a change in mindset); our schools need to respond to both. The technical challenges are daunting, since the new paradigm obviously calls for teaching a completely new set of skills in order to be effective learners in a world of infinite knowledge. But the adaptive challenge is even more overwhelming. As difficult as teaching new skills that we know little about may prove to be, the most radical change required is of a new collective approach to teaching, or rather to learning, that breaks away from many of our old, deeply ingrained conceptions of what teaching and learning are about, and that truly creates a new learning environment in which the learner is at the center. That is the only path to lifelong learning.

Like Moses leading his people, we must start by ascertaining that, even though we can see the "promised land," we are not ready to get there yet. We need to carefully break down and analyze the technical requirements—the new skills that are needed and how best to teach them; or rather, to learn them alongside our students. But, even more importantly, we need to go through a deeper process of soul-searching in our vocational calling, in our desire to be educators; we must be bold enough to leave no stone unturned in our quest to rediscover our own relationship with learning so that we, too, can be the new learners for this millennium.

A TALE OF TWO SCHOOLS

Claudia Wallis' cover article in the December 10, 2006, issue of *Time* magazine, "How to Bring Our Schools Out of the 20th Century," starts off with a cruel joke that takes a stab at schools and their inability to change and adapt to the new times.

It goes like this: Rip Van Winkle, the fictional character from Washington Irving's short story of the same name, falls asleep for 100 years shortly after the turn of the 20th century. He wakes up in the 21st century and finds that everything around him has changed in inconceivable ways—people are talking to each other on cell phones, automobiles and flying machines abound, and everywhere he goes he is completely bewildered and cannot understand anything that is going on. But then he enters a building and exclaims joyfully "Ah! I know what this is; this is a school! We had them in our time, only then the boards were black instead of green."

Generalizations are intrinsically unfair, but even so, there is an element of truth to this unflattering story about schools. Technology has dramatically changed almost every aspect of everyday life, and decisively influenced the workplace. We have already highlighted the profound changes that the advances in technology have spurred in the ways in which we can learn and effectively collaborate. Schools, however, have managed to remain largely immune to the massive onslaught of the technology wave, and the field of education is in many ways, like Rip Van Winkle, blissfully unaware that we live in a new world.

This tendency has been evident for some time, as reflected in a paper written by Stanford professor Larry Cuban back in 1993. The title of the paper is quite explicit: "Computers Meet Classroom: Classroom Wins." Throughout the paper, which now looms over educators as a self-fulfilled prophecy of sorts, a thorough analysis is made of the many reasons why super-rigid school structures coupled with unchangeable conceptions of what is right in teaching and learning provide an environment that is counterproductive to the development of computer-based applications for education.

As of now, we can argue about the extent and degree of the failure, but it cannot be disputed that the implementation of technology in the classroom is, at best, still a work in progress and that the long-promised benefits that technology can offer in transforming education are yet to be seen. A profound paradox emerges if we consider that the most significant impact of the advances in technology has been the fundamental and far-reaching changes in the conception of knowledge, enabling future generations to learn in better and unprecedented ways, and yet schools have erected themselves as the last bastions of the pre-Internet world.

Why is it that schools have resisted change so steadfastly, and how can we go about generating that change? There is no simple answer to either of these two pivotal questions. The cornerstone of change is the deep conviction that it is an inexorable way forward. And try as we might to remain impervious to the new world and the new society, there are driving forces for change that will sweep schools and education. It is better to meet them head on, and on our own terms. But in order to do that, we need to engage in a little soul-searching.

THE OLD SCHOOL

The school in which I work is, as of this writing, 172 years old. The walls of one of our meeting rooms feature some photographs of students and teachers from around a century earlier. I sometimes use those pictures in my presentations to jump-start a discussion on the old school. What really stands out from the photographs are the faces. Schoolmasters invariably glare at the photographer with very angry faces, and the students' expressions seem to oscillate between sadness and fear, epitomizing what was clearly the norm in human relationships at school at that time. (Educators have joked that in some schools, similar photographs taken now would show the exact opposite—sad, fearful teachers and angry students.)

Fortunately, that oppressive environment has gradually given way to more humane schools, with improved relationships between instructors and students. However, many of the underlying structures that provided the foundations for that type of school are still largely in place.

The event that clearly separated the old from the new school in our subsequent analysis is the invention and widespread use of the Internet. What we will now call the "old school" refers to schools in the pre-Internet era, which is still the predominant model in many schools and districts. The past tense in the list of old-school characteristics that follows can easily be replaced by a painful present tense in many cases.

The general underlying characteristics of the old school are directly linked to the previous knowledge paradigm:

- **Possessing knowledge had value:** Sir Francis Bacon said "knowledge is power," and the traditional educational system relied heavily on the acquisition of and, more often than not, the memorization of knowledge. Knowledge was physically centralized, in schools, universities, libraries, and other centers of learning, and people with no access to them were prevented from learning.

- **There was a content-based curriculum:** It follows logically that school curricula were predominantly focused on content. A cumulative sequencing of that content was the road to higher-order learning, and was also a prerequisite to progressing along successive courses of study.
- **Core subjects dominated the curriculum:** A heavy emphasis on the languages, mathematics, and, to a lesser extent, science as core subjects underscored the need to acquire certain basic central knowledge as an essential condition for learning the rest.
- **Higher studies consisted of specialization:** Gradually, as students progressed through the years, subjects became more and more specific in the complexity of the knowledge acquired, as an essential prerequisite to university studies, which in turn narrowed down the focus of specialization even further.
- **The teacher was at the center:** Because of the emphasis on content and a model of information scarcity, the teacher role was preeminent. Thus, teachers started off from an automatic position of self-invested power stemming out of the fact that they were the sole possessors of knowledge, so learning was heavily dependent on the teacher involved. This could be especially painful in elementary school, where a single teacher had complete power over the learners, and the proficiency of the instructor determined whether children lost or gained a year of learning at school. There was a yearly ritual of parents breathlessly awaiting the moment when teaching assignments were announced to learn whether their sons or daughters would be in the classrooms of "good" or "bad" teachers. The parents knew that this simple administrative decision could have a major impact on their child's life.

- **There was an overwhelming focus on reading and writing:**
  Since the almost exclusive medium for transmitting and
  sharing knowledge was the book and other written texts,
  reading (decoding that knowledge) and writing were the main
  skills to be acquired and perfected over the years. Despite the
  fact that many students, even though they had other talents,
  were unable to master these skills to the level required and
  therefore were outcasts in the school system, success in school
  was heavily dependent on how well students could read and
  write. These two skills constituted the Holy Grail of education, not only in that they held the key to learning in all
  subjects, but also in that they helped develop analytical skills
  that were deemed essential for the learning process in general.

- **Learning was almost always assessed by performance on sit-
  down written tests:** In their various "flavors" and "colors,"
  written tests were almost the only way to assess whether
  students were benefiting from instruction and progressing
  according to the school mission. Evaluation at school consisted
  of a seemingly endless sequence of written tests, and students
  gradually perfected their mastery of test-taking. Teachers in
  this environment were faced daily with students' ageless battle
  cry when attempting to present any topic: "Will this be on the
  test?" As they progressed through school, a sort of evolutionary
  process took place, and students became uncannily able to
  maximize their efficiency, learning only what was required to
  score well on tests. Standardized tests, measuring certain
  dimensions of the learning of vast numbers of students for
  comparison and benchmarking purposes, were particularly
  maligned, in that they became the quintessential measure,
  however inadequate, of scores-driven instruction. They
  stressed out teachers and students alike, not to mention
  administrators, who operated under the threat of school
  sanctions if scores did not improve. Once again, students who
  did not perform well under these conditions found themselves
  hopelessly ostracized in schools, at risk of being labeled as

learning disabled and sent away to be dealt with by special education teachers, in a process that, despite the best efforts of these specialists, irreparably undermined their self esteem.

- **Students were always grouped by age:** Sir Ken Robinson, a renowned school reform advocate and creativity specialist who has lately gained rock star status in the world of education, illustrates clearly an issue that has been taken for granted in the school system—that students should be grouped by age in nearly impermeable grade levels—when he says that school structure orders students exclusively by "date of manufacture" (Robinson, 2006). Ability, learning style, and interests, save in specific learning environments seen as reform efforts, have no bearing whatsoever on the way students are grouped to engage in learning.

- **Students were expected to learn material "on time":** It was common for teachers to admonish their students to study for the test in such a way that they knew all the material on a certain day. Mastering content and skills within the time frame that fits the sequencing specified by the teacher was more important than the learning itself. When students who did not perform well clamored for a retest, or some other form of assessment that gave them more time or a second chance to master their learning, any teacher who agreed was accused of being a pushover. Schools created an artificial cowboy duel culture in which students had one chance to draw and fire, and if they missed, they suffered the consequences.

- **Progress was calculated using averages:** Within an environment in which grades ruled, marks that determined the success of students at school were determined in most cases by calculating an average that included complicated weighting formulas. Thus, generally, a single failure during the grading period represented an indelible blemish for students, even if they eventually became proficient in the material. End-of-term summative examinations added to the dramatic make-or-break scenario: they determined whether a student received a passing grade, or at least contributed heftily towards the final average. Students who progressed well throughout the grading period could have a single "bad day" that drastically affected their final grade. Jay Cross, in his seminal book *Informal Learning* (2006), is quite drastic in dismissing the exacerbated importance assigned to grades. He calls it "academia's deep, dark secret: outside of the school system, grades are meaningless."

• **Mistakes were not allowed:** Mistakes were stigmatized in the learning process. It is widely known and well accepted that trial and error and learning from one's own mistakes is a secure path for learning and acquiring proficiency, especially in a fail-safe environment like the one that schools can provide, where mistakes are inconsequential and not detrimental to learning. Despite this, schools have instituted an implicitly repressive environment that progressively stifles students' creativity, curiosity, and spontaneity for fear of being ridiculed. (Chess grand master Aron Nimzowitsch transcended the game with his statement that a threat is stronger than the realization of that threat.) One all-too-common conduct that teachers observe in children of all ages is that they appear to be disengaged and literally "switch off" because they would much rather be labeled as lazy than be considered dumb.

• **Knowledge was meticulously compartmentalized:** The subject structure was pervasive in schools, especially at the high school or secondary level. Learning was rigorously classified into subjects, and little or no interaction was encouraged between different subjects and departments. Interdisciplinary projects were rare events, reserved to the realm of progressive or experimental programs.

• **There were clear and well-defined outcomes that indicated academic success:** The old school had very clear markers for success, based on the Gaussian curve (or bell curve) that separated those who were academically able from those who were not (and who were sometimes explicitly referred to as "learning disabled"). Schools needed to produce graduates who would be able to succeed in a predominantly left-brained analytical world where knowledge and precisely defined core skills were paramount to progressing in university studies and gaining a secure foothold in the workplace. The market demanded specialists, and prospective employers were more interested in proficiency than in potential.

The preceding attempt to objectively dissect and expose the underlying basic premises under which the old school operated reinforces the need for change. Most of the bare-bones facts about school systems seem to be at cross purposes with the new knowledge paradigm and the changes taking place. But it would be naïve to think that teachers and educational leaders have conspired over the years to create schools that would remain immune to the passage of time and would operate in denial of current trends. But however unintentional it was, the reality that needs to be faced is that schools have not kept up with the times.

The first step in trying to modify the prevailing mindset is to acknowledge that there are deeply embedded convictions about what is right and wrong in education, and that they have given rise to a model that seems to have become woefully inadequate. These lists of "old-school" and "new-school" characteristics are intended as a sobering wake-up call to the magnitude of the changes that have to be implemented if we are to reform schools in a way that makes them meaningful and relevant in the 21st century. But this is just the beginning of the story.

THE NEW SCHOOL

Whenever we think about the "new school" we are immediately tempted to think in terms of technology and modern buildings. However, despite the fact that modern building design and the introduction of technology seem to be the icons of change, it is clear that what we can see is only the tip of the iceberg, and that the real and more profound changes that are needed are somewhat more intangible but far more important.

In many cases, the main features of the "new school" and the characteristics of the old school are mutually exclusive:

- **Lifelong learning is the primary goal of the educational system:** The possibility of accessing infinite knowledge with just a few keystrokes and the incontrovertible fact that the Internet has become a limitless repository of knowledge have forever changed the fundamental premise of teaching and learning. In the present, and to an almost unimaginable extent in the near future, anybody will be able to learn everything that the best researchers in the field know about any topic or theme. Contrary to the old paradigm, in which knowledge needed to be acquired from finite sources and remembered, in the new scenario the most important skill by far is to be able to efficiently and effectively find, sort through, and learn from the abundance of information that is available. After being a "wishful thinking" phrase included in most school mission statements for ages, "lifelong learning" has become a feasible reality, and educators are being challenged to take those words on the wall and make them the main objective of the educational system.

- **Education is more about learning than teaching:** Contrary to some of the deepest conceptions about schooling, the most important and relevant process in schools is not teaching, but learning. Education was synonymous with teaching, and the focus of all efforts was and often still is centered on refining teaching techniques, with the explicit goal of getting content and skills across to the learners, based on the assumption that learning takes place mostly within the formal environment of schools. Lifelong learning inevitably alters the landscape. If we need to prepare our students to continue learning for life without teachers around who will provide access to that knowledge, the educational process necessarily has to shift the focus onto the learner. A new pedagogy needs to reassess the need to develop these lifelong learning skills, centering much more on the learning process and on how students will be able to learn for the rest of their lives utilizing the resources available. (Interestingly, the word *pedagogy*, associated now with the process of teaching, is derived from the Greek *paidagogos*, which refers to a servant who made sure children went to school and did their homework.)

- **Every child can learn:** Despite the many astounding technological advances and substantial improvements in education in general, perhaps the greatest finding of the 21st century is that every child can learn. Contrary to the deeply ingrained model of the Gaussian curve that separated the capable from the incapable, it is now accepted by most education experts, including Howard Gardner (1983) with his theory of multiple intelligences, that every child has a different learning style and that it is no longer on the student's shoulders to adapt to a one-size-fits-all model of schooling. Instead—and this constitutes a massive cultural shift—schools have to provide for each student and assume responsibility for every child's success. Coming from a model in which students had to learn in the ways and times mandated by the teacher, or not learn at all ("My way or the highway!"), this fundamental change brings forth an unprecedented challenge. The adjustments needed to effect this change are not just cosmetic modifications of teaching methods, but a complete overhauling of the present system to tailor instruction to the needs of each student. Needless to say, this student-centric approach requires that teachers fill a completely different role than the one they were trained for. Even more importantly, some teachers may have chosen the profession based on a hopelessly outdated job description.

- **Our students are different from us:** Neuroscience is still an emerging science, but many experts are asserting that the very

different stimuli that the younger generation is being
exposed to will result in their brains being wired differently
(www.earthsky.org, www.nimh.nih.gov). The current generation of students has developed in a digital world that
bombards them with a multiplicity of inputs. Consequently,
our students are different from the ones that the educational
system prepared us to teach. They have developed different
thinking patterns and learning styles, and the old tools in the
teachers' toolboxes are insufficient to deal with them. Marc
Prensky's (2001) digital natives and immigrants metaphor is a
good example of one dimension of the challenge: adults'
relationship with the digital world is a skill that has been, at
best, learned late in life, and therefore it will always surface
with an "accent" that betrays the feeble and fragile nature of
the knowledge, just as immigrants who learn a new language
as adults might speak it with grammatically correct phrases,
but will never speak it like native speakers.

• **Customized education is necessary:** Largely because of
expected outcomes that were anchored in what were deemed
to be indisputable indicators for success according to the
industry model, schooling was, and still largely is, delivered in
a homogeneous, one-size-fits-all style that does not cater to
the particular needs and learning styles of each individual. If
we operate under the axiom that every child can succeed and
that the school should work on detecting each child's talents,
it is obvious that the educational system must become
increasingly customized to meet the needs of every child. As
soon as we realize the implications of the previous statement
and compare it to the current system of standardized tests and
universally applied methods, we can grasp the magnitude of
the change required, not only in teaching strategies, but also
in the more profound philosophical approach that entails
humbling ourselves to find the best way to develop the talent
of every child, and not expecting them, explicitly or implicitly,

to conform to external parameters that define successful learning.

- **New skills need to be taught:** Beyond the deeper philosophical issues that call out for a new pedagogy, there is a dire need to start teaching some of the new skills associated with the 21st-century model of teaching and learning. There are various frameworks and taxonomies to this effect, but regardless of the specific breakdown of these skills and what we call them, the completely different nature of the knowledge model based on infinite abundance, the limitless availability of digital content that includes multimedia, unprecedented opportunities for collaboration, and a 24-hours-a-day, seven-days-a-week, 365-days-a-year connected world redefines the skills that need to be taught at schools. Just to give one example, an essential skill in the current scenario is the ability to search for information, filter it, distinguish what is relevant from what is not, and spot erroneous or biased content amidst an overabundance of data. Schools largely expect students to acquire these skills by themselves, and mistakenly assume that taking students to the computer lab and telling them how to search in Google is enough. Our evaluations are always meticulously designed so that they include all the information that students have been told to study—not more, not less. Math and science students often bemoan the existence of a single extra piece of data in a numeric problem that they do not need for its solution. If we want them to develop an almost intuitive capacity for weeding out unneeded or wrong data, we should, for instance, as a simple and direct measure, from a very early stage in the educational process, make sure that all tests and evaluations contain more data than needed, and that, occasionally, some of it is either erroneous or biased.

- **Learning is ubiquitous:** Another marked difference in the new school from the norm in the old school is that learning does not take place only within the classroom. Extracurricular activities, sports, drama, art and music programs, just to name a few of the most common options that schools currently offer, will no longer be viewed as add-ons, but rather as integral and essential components within the educational process. A new curriculum must explicitly address learning opportunities that take place outside of the classroom and restructure the school day so that these other interactions are scheduled in order to achieve the learning objectives of the school.

• **Brain-based learning techniques will become more prevalent:** Researchers are gaining ground in terms of new pedagogies and educational theories in all areas, but by far the "killer app" when it comes to practical applications for the classroom has to do with neuro-developmental research. As researchers learn more and more about the inner mechanisms of the brain and how humans learn and acquire knowledge, we can expect to see mainstream implementations of this theory make their way into classroom practice. At this point, some software (most notably Fast ForWord reading software, which is based on neurocognitive research) is already available and proving to be effective, but most real-life applications are in the early stages or still under development. As the natural extension of a customized education system, brain-based learning promises to deliver not only the best teaching approach for each learning style, but also an improved capacity to learn through early stimulation and scientific assessment of each student's talents and abilities.

• **Different learning environments will be utilized:** Even though the introduction of technology and physical changes in the school buildings are the least important changes needed in the 21st-century environment, it is still true that the new school will have a very different layout. Technology will have a far greater presence, and all students will, in the near future, use their own personalized computing devices that will allow them to connect to the Internet. Harvard professor Richard Elmore (2006) notes that the ambiance in most corporations and businesses provides clear messages about their products and their corporate image, and that in schools, the current disposition of most classrooms also, regretfully, betrays the way in which we conduct business: student desks rigidly face the front, where the teacher stands at the center. We can expect that schools not only will have modified curriculums, but also will look different in order to provide appropriate spaces for this different paradigm.

This list of new-school characteristics could literally go on forever. These characteristics are not intended to be a laundry list of themes to be tackled, but they underscore the fundamental differences between the old school and the new school, and the magnitude of the changes needed.

Any exercise in envisioning the future will draw attention to the abyss between the current educational system and what the future will bring into our classrooms. The formidable task that teachers, administrators, and policy makers are faced with is trying to provide ways for our students to become productive citizens in this not-so-new century.

CHAPTER TWO

Curriculum
for the Future

I F WE DON'T WANT THE 21ST-CENTURY-SKILLS MOVEMENT to become
another casualty of educational skepticism, a radical change is
needed in our approach to implementing a new pedagogy. Despite
all that has been written about the need to teach completely new skills,
classrooms are still more "old school" than "new school."

Efforts so far have largely targeted the teaching of a new taxonomy
of skills that are unique to the new knowledge paradigm of infinite
abundance and the successful introduction of technology into the classroom. However, part of the reason for the sense of futility that seems to
accompany any major attempt at educational reform is related to the
focus of the reform and the way educators approach its implementation.

The most significant hurdle to be overcome has to do with the way
we go about professional development. The intrinsic complexity of the
21st-century-infinite-knowledge paradigm and the open-ended nature
of the challenge we face do not allow for a left-brained, all-encompassing
sequential approach to implementing change.

Embracing the latest one-size-fits-all trend or educational theory is
a common, but woefully inadequate, approach to professional development when trying to implement 21st-century skills, which by definition are of a dynamic nature and require customized implementation.

As much as we would like to buy an off-the-shelf solution and continue relying on outside experts to supply us with bulletproof recipes
for success, the answer lies within each school and district, and the most
that can be done via external facilitation is identifying the main themes

to address and the questions to be asked, so that we can target the areas that clearly need reform. The complexity of the task at hand can be difficult to handle, but, paradoxically, it can also have a freeing effect: the anguish of trying to apply third-party highly prescriptive methods that are not suited to each classroom's reality can gradually be diffused when teachers use strategies that are specifically designed to fit their needs.

STARTING POINTS

Connie Kamm refers in her presentations to an analogy from futurist Glen Hiemstra, in his book *Turning the Future into Revenue* (2006), to describe the effect of the 21st century on education: There are some railroad tracks with no bells or flashing lights, just a sign that says that the train will cross the tracks at a certain time, regardless of whether we are there or not. We can choose to jump on the train or remain behind. Schools can choose to turn their backs on change, but change will continue, driven by forces that are stronger than our individual efforts, and beyond our control.

Where does this train take us? If we go a little deeper in the gap analysis between this uncertain but unstoppable future and our current schools, despite acknowledging the need for customized solutions, we can address the main areas that need profound reform as a necessary first step.

The Teacher Mindset

In the old pedagogy-of-poverty model, the teacher possessed and administered knowledge, and as such was automatically at the center of everything in the classroom. Since learning emanated from the teacher, it was only natural that profuse lecturing would be the norm. Even when using other resources, such as textbooks or other teaching aids, it would still be the teacher who, through carefully crafted assignments and evaluations, would set the pace and, more importantly, the expected outcomes for learning. What these teachers were doing, ultimately, was teaching to their own self-image—they were accepting as universal a unique model for successful learning that was based on their own learning style.

The teacher's role in the old school was one of almost absolute self-invested power over the students, not only in terms of classroom discipline (which was linked to some degree to instruction that was not tailored to students' learning styles, causing disruptive behavior by students), but also through the use of grading as a weapon, since it was the exclusive prerogative of the teacher to decide when learning had been achieved.

Lifelong learning as a primary and overarching goal, a student-centered pedagogy, and tailoring instruction to each student's needs necessitate that teachers have a completely different role. Rather than embodying knowledge and demanding that students learn the way the teachers dictates they should, teachers need to humble themselves and become more like mentors, role models, and coaches for their students. One-on-one interactions will be more frequent, and the teacher's role will not be to dispense knowledge, but rather to guide and facilitate students' learning. Each individual will have a personalized learning plan and objectives, based on standards and related skills and contents, and teachers must become partners with students to help them achieve those goals. The coaching model is an apt one, in that it explicitly places the responsibility of attaining the learning objectives and success on both the student and the teacher, as opposed to the old-school setting, in which learning is entirely the responsibility of the students, and success depends on whether they make the passing grade or standard.

This required change in role is especially difficult because it gnaws at some of the very reasons why many people in the profession chose it. Most of us teachers love to lecture, love to hear our own voices, love to be in control of learning, and have grown to enjoy those moments in which we manage to get across a difficult concept to the whole class. And some teachers still relish their position of power over students, and, regretfully, abuse their authority with extremely negative consequences. This negative trend manifests itself in a number of ways, but particularly through the use of grading practices that not only negatively affect student learning, but, in some cases, do irreparable damage to children's and adolescents' intrinsically fragile self-esteem.

Even though it's tough, this transition to the role of mentor can be very rewarding in terms of building up stronger bonds and closer personal relationships with students, relationships that have always been at the real heart of education.

Skills versus Content

Another fundamental change that schools have to work on is the implicit and explicit underlying emphasis of most curricula on content. It is undeniable that content must be an important and integral part of the curriculum, since you cannot use high-order thinking skills on what is not known, and, eventually, students must exit school as well-informed citizens who possess a solid cultural base. However, the almost exclusive focus on concatenated cumulative content that is the norm in most school-based and standardized programs of study must gradually give way to one that is centered on the acquisition of the skills needed for the new school.

The increasingly transient nature of knowledge also calls for a different approach to instruction. Although core knowledge remains as an unalterable foundation for the curriculum, the level of specificity needs to be reassessed in light of the fact that new information is generated at breathtaking speed and some of the content taught may become outdated or obsolete very quickly. Rather than attaining a high degree of specialization in subject areas, the foremost goal of a new curriculum should be to prepare students to be able to further their knowledge according to their interests or future work.

The preeminence of content as the driving factor in curriculum decisions is also now in question. In the past, courses of study were drawn up with outcomes in mind that addressed mostly what students should know and understand, with skills acquired as almost a byproduct of the process, but the current scenario inverts those priorities—specific content needs to be chosen based on how it can effectively advance the teaching of the skills needed, and not the other way round.

A two-tiered decision-making process is then needed to determine curriculum content: (1) which core content must be taught in order to provide a good cultural base and background to be fully functional in the 21st century, and (2) which content is best suited to act as a catalyst for the teaching of skills that address the 21st-century challenge, with the ultimate goal of generating lifelong learners?

In an educational world in which curriculum decisions are either externally mandated or made in automatic-pilot mode, asking these questions and attempting to answer them constitutes a formidable challenge, since there are no standard processes and structures in place at schools and districts to address them, and such structures and processes will be essential to effecting the desired changes.

Assessment

If I were to choose one single area in which to start an educational reform process based on how outdated it is and the projected impact of changes, it would undoubtedly be assessment.

Even in schools that have started improvement processes that are aimed at reshaping teaching and learning practices to better suit the 21st century, assessment still constitutes an Achilles' heel. Whether we like it or not, it is also a fact that, despite our best-intentioned efforts to emphasize the intrinsic value of learning, students will largely respond to the way we evaluate, and will continue to ask, "Will this be on the test?"

And that single phrase hints in itself at the extent and nature of the problem regarding assessment. On the one hand, it refers explicitly and unequivocally to the test. Despite years of educational seminars, hundreds of books dedicated to breaking down the nature and goals of assessment, and a clearly discernible movement towards formative assessment, the vast majority of assessments in school systems all over the world and in every age group are still sit-down, fixed-time, end-of-unit written tests with no second chances. Students often request retesting when they do not succeed during the original evaluation, but because of stringent demands to comply with the mandated curriculum in the given time, those requests are generally met with indifference by teachers who are tired of grading and would not even consider offering a second evaluation.

Most of these summative end-of-the-road evaluations are focused on content rather than skills, and more often than not, a substantial emphasis is placed on factual recall.

But our educational system is supposed to prepare students for real life, and it is easy to see that this artificial assessment model has little resemblance to reality. In real life, there are almost no one-chance do-or-die scenarios, and whenever anybody has to demonstrate proficiency in any field, the timing for demonstrating that competency is chosen by the candidate, rather than being an arbitrary date set in stone.

When a driver's license is issued, allowing a person to operate a potentially lethal object (the car) in a social context where it could physically harm others, the issuing body wants to ensure that the driver has acquired the skills necessary to drive the car responsibly and safely. It does not really matter how many times the candidate tries; it only matters that the driver has perfected those skills before being issued a license.

Thomas Guskey (2007) mentions that the two closest real-life examples of critical applications where mistakes are not allowed and human beings must make very complex decisions in the blink of an eye are probably surgeons and astronauts. In both cases, they do not gain their qualifications by means of written tests, but through an extensive program of simulations and mentoring and apprenticeship with experts. The current testing system goes out of the way to penalize and stigmatize mistakes, but, for example, in the moon program, which is still thought of as one of the greatest technical accomplishments in history, astronauts were drilled over and over in all types of failure scenarios, and they recall that their best learning occurred from the failed attempts at landing in the simulations.

Dylan Wiliam (2008) equates end-of-unit summative assessment to an airline pilot addressing the passengers and telling them that they will be on the ground in a few minutes and only then will they be able to ascertain which airport they have landed at. If it is the wrong destination, there is nothing that can be done about it at that point.

Standardized testing adds insult to injury: for the sake of having external objective measures of the progress of schools and students and the degree of attainment of standards, a universal evaluation is administered to all students, regardless of their individual circumstances and learning styles. Even worse, important educational decisions are made based on those results, including, in some cases, the closure of schools.

Feedback from the teacher given after it is "too late," even when it is not delayed by lags in grading due to work overload, does not serve the purpose of schooling—to engender learning. The combination of an artificial environment, the finality of most instruments of assessment, and the perception that evaluation is not linked to learning all conspire towards making assessment a loaded weapon in the hands of the teacher. Sadly, some educators relish this explicit power to literally rule over the lives of their students and, abusing this prerogative, they do substantial harm not only to students under their charge, but also to the public's view of education in general.

Educators acknowledge in whispers what is loud and clear, that our current assessment system is fundamentally flawed and intrinsically counterproductive to many of the accepted principles of education and to the modern-day challenge of reshaping our schools for the 21st century.

Where can we find clues about how to create a more legitimate and authentic assessment system? Douglas Reeves (2007b) provides us with a relevant example of what works: video games. Younger children and adolescents do not need any prompting from adults to spend inordinate amounts of time seemingly transfixed, eyes glued to the computer screen, playing video games. At first glance, it is tempting to attribute these semi-addictive levels of engagement solely to the playful nature of the games themselves, but if we look at the underlying characteristics and nature of the interactions that students have when engaged in the games, some other reasons help to explain the success of gaming and the lessons we can learn from it.

Novice users learn the basics of the task at hand through tutorials that generally walk them through the set of core skills needed to progress in the game. As soon as they feel that they have a basic toolbox mastered, they start to play the game right away, completely unafraid of making mistakes. In most games, players are allowed to choose characters based on their preferences and game-related traits. They can only move on to more complex scenarios once they have completed previous levels, but there is no time limit to achieve this, and there are unlimited opportunities to do it. Moving through the game, they are able to open up new levels and collect tokens and special items and abilities for their characters, who thus mirror their improved capacities, and there are no telltale scars that betray the number of failures or lives lost in previous levels.

When gamers lose, in most cases their characters are literally killed. But instead of crying "unfair" and giving up, they start again, and they doggedly keep on trying until they can progress on to the next stage.

It sounds like a dream scenario for education: full engagement, students learning at their own individual pace, immediate and relevant feedback, no fixed time in which to complete the learning objectives, unlimited opportunities, a safe environment to make mistakes, rewards that provide an incentive to progress and that build up students' self-esteem, progressive mastering of increasingly complicated skills and content, and a personalized learning environment.

Even though there is huge potential for the use of gaming in education, what transcends this fact is that these characteristics that make games so attractive to young people are almost exactly the opposite of the way in which we evaluate them. We can wish that there were more state-of-the-art realistic games that have valid educational content, but we can also attempt to reshape our assessment system to mirror some of the features of games in order to make gains in relevance and authenticity.

It might be argued that the current teacher-to-student ratio in most schools makes much of this unfeasible, but it is interesting to look back to the first schools, and what still happens in isolated rural areas, where teachers single-handedly operate one-room schools in which children of different ages coexist in their learning. Because of the difference in ages, teachers do no lecturing, and focus their efforts on providing almost personalized instruction to each student. The evolution of small schools into larger ones and the grouping of students by age led to the "sage on the stage" role for teachers that clearly prevents them from engaging in the one-to-one interactions that are implicit in the gaming model. Technology and computers can clearly facilitate the process, but it is, once again, the change in the role and prevailing mindset of the teachers that will spur these long-overdue changes.

Whole-Child Learning

Another direct, and very positive, consequence of the realization that every child has a unique potential to be fulfilled is the awareness that the educational process must go far beyond academic instruction to encompass character formation and the building of a set of skills that are more than just academic standards.

Many authors have highlighted how the current educational system only caters to the academic dimension of learning, and that everything in schools, from how we teach to the way we think to how we structure professional development and adult learning, is designed to suit that dimension. Sir Ken Robinson, in his groundbreaking book *The Element: How Finding Your Passion Changes Everything* (2009), specifically addresses this issue: "The current systems also put severe limits on how teachers teach and students learn. Academic ability is very important, but so are other ways of thinking. People who think visually might love a particular topic or subject, but won't realize it if their teachers only present it in one, nonvisual way. Yet our education systems increasingly encourage teachers to teach students in a uniform fashion."

Daniel Pink, in his book *A Whole New Mind* (2006), very clearly analyzes how the complexity of the 21st century and the limitless data of the knowledge era completely invalidate the left-brained analytical model, and notes that corporations are even seeking leaders that come from fields such as the arts, because those individuals' right-brained holistic comprehension of a very complex reality can provide the global vision that is needed to move forward in this era.

From statewide standards all the way down to compartmentalized subject structure, our schools are explicitly designed to perpetuate the academic nature of learning. Rewards and incentives are built into the system to guide students towards rigid expected outcomes, and they reward achievement and results.

Moving away from absolute parameters in all respects, a greater emphasis on a holistic education that is focused on the whole child goes hand-in-hand with the changes suggested in the preceding points, and is a major cultural change in the needed reform.

A NEW CURRICULUM
FOR THE DIGITAL AGE

The teaching of new skills, lifelong learning as the overarching goal of schooling, and a completely new paradigm also call out for a new curriculum that leaves no stone unturned and that dares to challenge some sacrosanct assumptions that the educational system has been operating on for ages.

Even though the changes are far-reaching, the methods are yet to be discerned, and, as befits the new paradigm, each school and district will eventually have to come up with its own local answers to this global problem, there are several salient aspects of the curriculum that come into focus when designing a true 21st-century curriculum.

The Hierarchy of Subjects

The needs of an industrial world were the key to determining the priorities of the content being taught at schools. Students after graduation were expected to be fully functional, to be able to take jobs, and a fraction of them to move on to higher studies in college. In a more predictable world, with standard predetermined outcomes for success, the industry and service sectors clearly delimited the core subjects that were needed to acquire the knowledge and skills that the workplace demanded.

This naturally led to a hierarchy of subjects, based on their usefulness relative to the model. What we now accept without a second thought as the core subjects constitute the building blocks of knowledge tailored to perfectly compartmentalized objectives: mathematics as the foundation for computing and accounting, reading and writing as the default means of expression, history as a conduit to emphasizing a mostly facts-based awareness of cultural heritage, and, to a lesser extent, the sciences to supply the theoretical foundations of industrial processes.

The rest of the subjects were, at best, viewed as supplements to provide students with some cultural background or to expose them to career paths related to fields like art, drama, music, or sports. The reason for the relative value of subjects within the curriculum was, of course, their degree of usefulness in the context of the pre-Internet model of teaching, focused mostly on content. If we accept the emergence of a new paradigm that is based on skills and that has lifelong learning as its ultimate goal, we can reassess the role of each of the subjects, taking into account how they contribute to providing a cultural base and, essentially, to the building of skills.

The traditional hierarchy of subjects no longer reflects the skill set required by a far-more-complex scenario involving staggering amounts of data that cannot be encompassed analytically, and it does not take into account the existence of tools and technologies that truly redefine some mental processes and move them towards a more formative role. Nontraditional subjects can suddenly be reconsidered, not in terms of their absolute value, since in the new school there are no standard outcomes for success, but rather in terms of the skills their teaching will foster.

An example that immediately comes to mind is that of mathematics and art. Near the top of the hierarchy of subjects in the old school, mathematics has long dominated the curriculum based on the need to develop students' analytical abilities as well as to provide them with a necessary platform from which to learn science, technology and engineering, traditional building blocks of the industrial 20th-century world. At the base of the old-school academic hierarchy, we find art. In a purely utilitarian model, art is relegated to the role of aesthetic entertainment, and, for those gifted enough, as a means of expression. Because it served no specific purpose within the old-school set of exit skills to succeed in the post-school world, it followed almost inevitably that the time allocated to art would be proportionally much less and, as students moved up into the higher grades, became an optional or extracurricular activity.

But now things are different. Ubiquitous technology and miniaturization have rendered some mathematical skills superfluous, and the analytical abilities associated with learning mathematics are no longer as essential as they were, given a scenario of ever-increasing complexity that no longer can be encompassed analytically. On the other hand, the skills that can be derived from an artistic education are tailor-made for the 21st century. Right-brain drawing courses proliferate, and corporate executives can't get enough of them—they are trying to gain a more holistic approach to problem solving.

The purpose and role of these two subjects have changed in the face of the new knowledge paradigm, and even though I am not for a minute suggesting that math should be done away with or anything of the sort, without entering into the time allocation realm, the way math and art are taught should be reevaluated in a true 21st-century curriculum.

Reassessing the hierarchy and role of each of the subjects, and even the degree of separation of disciplines in the school curriculum, should be a primary consideration in the analysis of the changes needed.

LANGUAGES AND EXPRESSION

Once again, at the risk of engaging in educational blasphemy at the mere suggestion of such a shift, a new curriculum should also deemphasize the almost obsessive current focus on reading and writing. Before passing judgment about whether we dare mess with literacy, which has until now been the Holy Grail of education, we should evaluate the context in which we function in the present and what the future will surely bring.

The undisputed dominance of reading and writing as the ultimate skills to be taught and as the embodiment of academic proficiency had its origin in the fact that the written word was the exclusive medium for communicating and transmitting knowledge. Within that scenario, it did make sense that perfecting the ability to decode (reading comprehension) and write was hailed as the most important goal in education, even surpassing numeracy in the hierarchy, to the not-often-recognized detriment of students' oral skills.

But we now live in a completely different world. Young people have grown up in a multimedia-rich environment, and regardless of our zeal for extolling the virtues of reading, they will be consuming many more sounds, images, and videos than texts. Marc Prensky, in his landmark article on "Digital Natives" (2001), cites the following related statistics:

"Today's average college grads have spent less than 5,000 hours of their lives reading, but over 10,000 hours playing video games (not to mention 20,000 hours watching TV)."

Regardless of the specific numbers, to a certain extent this also holds true for most functioning adults. Inasmuch as schools and international examination boards still demand the 4,000-word essay as a graduation requirement, it constitutes, at best, an exercise which is reserved for the world of academics, and even in that case with increasing infrequency. Both in the academic world and the real world (and those two worlds should not be mutually exclusive) the de facto means of expression is the multimedia presentation. Even in the realm of academia, lengthy dissertations have yielded to more dynamic and engaging multimedia presentations.

In effect, the much-maligned PowerPoint presentation and all its related siblings are what most adults have to develop, both in the workplace and the classroom. And most of us find that, save for scattered instructional efforts geared at mastering commands in computer science classes, we are absolutely ill-prepared to deliver our ideas through that medium, combining videos, sounds, images, text, and our oral presentation.

This is widely known, even among educators, but nothing is done about it. How to express ideas through multimedia design, which should be regarded as a basic skill at this point, is not explicitly and systematically taught to students in most schools.

Increasing the number of hours of literacy instruction has become the universal remedy for improving performance in schools, and the virtues of teaching writing and reading skills are not to be denied, both as applied to the skills themselves and in terms of their proven beneficial side effects on learning other disciplines. But we should at least ask ourselves, "At what expense do we focus so obsessively on reading and writing?"

The most overlooked issue in education is the opportunity cost implicit in curriculum decisions, and, consequently, many pertinent and relevant questions are never asked. What makes reading and writing rise an order of magnitude above all other means of expression?

Could we not devote some time to teaching students how to express their ideas using multimedia tools? Why is it that we think it is intrinsically useless to spend time consuming videos, music, Web pages, and other multimedia sources?

Students are drilled to death on reading comprehension tests, and, of all the abilities associated with reading and writing, we might argue that decoding text is still the most current, given the fact that there are vast amounts of text to be read on the Web. However, we never see a "video comprehension test," and our ability to "read between the lines" (note that our language reflects the predominance of reading and writing in our mindset) is even more needed in the case of multimedia, since there are many more subtle and easy-to-use tools that convey messages to consumers, both purposely and inadvertently.

Even though it remains largely unspoken, the main pedagogical support for the transcendence of reading and writing in the curriculum is that converting what is read into mind images, and the similar process of decoding mind images and converting them into writing, develops students' analytical abilities, imagination, and capacity to express abstractions. But now, though still in its infancy, there is research being done in the emerging field of visual literacy to develop a similar set of tools and skills to be learned in the classroom through the analysis and production of visual means of expression.

Reading and writing will still be central and relevant in a 21st-century curriculum, but it is imperative that schools gradually begin to shift some of the almost exclusive emphasis on them to teaching and learning how to consume and produce other media based on images, sounds, and video.

Handwriting: The Lost Art

Of all the anachronistic obsessions that still plague many school systems everywhere in the world, my favorite one is the teaching of handwriting. Even though in real life functioning adults will seldom have to write anything physically, a large percentage of schools still invest many instructional hours in having students painstakingly learn how to develop their cursive handwriting and devote hours to the meticulous drawing of each letter to the teacher's satisfaction.

It might be argued that handwriting is a good catalyst for the honing of fine motor skills, but a little online research reveals that, if that were the objective, there are far more efficient and targeted methods to help students improve their fine motor skills.

It is bad enough, in terms of opportunity costs, to think of the other skills and content that could be taught in some of the time devoted to handwriting. But handwriting as a make-or-break ability has also done indelible damage to the self-esteem of many children who, being perfectly able and capable of performing well in school, have been stigmatized and pushed into failure as a consequence of their poor handwriting. This judgmental educational attitude is grounded on prejudice and an intrinsically flawed model that places the entire responsibility on the shoulders of students, which is completely contradictory to the 21st-century realization that every child can learn.

NEW SKILLS

Substantial efforts have been made to create a taxonomy of the new skills required in modern times. Even though there is some common ground and consensus regarding the general scope of these skills, the deeply ingrained need to label and categorize these new skills is counter to the very complex and dynamic scenario in which they will be used.

For example, participation in a Webcast that includes interacting with an expert and students from other parts of the world could be classified as either collaboration, technological literacy, or globalization (to cite just a few of the most common categories). So which category does that exercise belong in? Clearly, it belongs in all of them, and it illustrates the futility of trying to sort multifaceted skills into strict, tidy categories.

But, regardless of what name we put to them or how we sort them, a new curriculum for the 21st century undoubtedly involves the teaching of some completely new skills that are required to succeed in a scenario of abundant knowledge.

Filtering

The most important skill in this new era is the ability to navigate successfully a seemingly overwhelming abundance of data, distinguishing what is relevant from what is not, and making good use of that information in the process.

Coming from an educational world in which students have been, for ages, spoon-fed all the knowledge they needed to accomplish the task at hand (and not a drop more), dealing with an infinite searchable database of available information requires skills that we are not teaching, and that transcend the mere act of refining searches in Google. Through systematic teaching of this skill from a very young age, we can aspire to help a new generation of students develop an instinctive sense for nonbiased, accurate, and relevant information, as well as the academic tools needed to formally validate knowledge and weed out information that is of no value.

Collaboration

Once I had to deliver a 10-minute presentation in front of an international examination board, in the context of an advisory conference that attempted to deliver insights into what the future would bring for education. Faced with the enormity of having to communicate so much in such precious little time, I opted to call in two former students of mine, and we role-played what the school of the future would be like.

Naturally, this short video included our "future" girls collaborating online with students from other parts of the world, and, in one instance in which they were comparing their own school lives with those of their parents, they discuss incredulously the fact that in the old days (today), students worked individually, whereas in their time (the future), if they were caught doing a project on their own they would be punished.

The advances in telecommunications and state-of-the-art authoring tools allow our generation to effectively collaborate in unprecedented ways, and, amongst others, the concept of augmented intelligence points to the increased collective capacity of work groups; there are now no barriers that limit the potential of collaboration.

In the same way that filtering needs to become second nature for our students, the ability to collaborate must also become an almost automatic skill in children. The concept of collaboration has been present in schools for decades, albeit approached in a lukewarm manner. There are specialized programs (i.e., Cooperative Learning) that are taught in professional development courses for teachers who want to learn about this pedagogical option. But rather than being an option for teachers, in a 21st-century curriculum, collaboration in learning must be the norm.

Globalization

The reality of the globalized world is beyond dispute. As we have already referenced, we now live in a flat world, a leveled playing field in which many of the traditional geographical and cultural barriers to international integration have been eliminated.

As a result of this dynamic scenario, functioning adults will be expected to interact with people from all over the world, both in the workplace and on a personal level. Jobs are increasingly outsourced, and the new economy calls for finding a relevant role for each individual to ensure that his or her job will not be eventually lost to the international competition. Our students are growing up in a global village and are being presented with models and examples that largely transcend their proximity to the examples set in their household, town, and even country.

The way to best deal with this situation is to work on developing a global mindset, but reinforcing students' identity within the local community. As with many other expected traits of the 21st-century citizen, our students are being expected to magically evolve into it.

Understanding the complexity of the new era, having an increased awareness of cultural factors that explicitly addresses foreign cultures, developing a strong sense of identity in the multicultural context, and honing the abilities needed to process seemingly infinite stimuli are only a few of the skills that must be present in a 21st-century curriculum. As with any skill, these must be progressively and systematically taught from a very early age.

Decisions need to be made involving the subject areas and content to include. For example, should there be a shift from physical geography, that is, the teaching of geographical features, which has traditionally been the core of that subject in schools, to a much greater emphasis on human geography, so that students can learn about the cultural and demographic aspects of each country? The answer in this case seems straightforward enough, but similar questions need to be asked in the other subject areas as well, so that the content to be included in the curriculum is geared towards the teaching of the desired skills, and not the other way round.

THE RISKS

So far, so good. We have extensively reviewed how the new paradigm challenges educators to develop new capacities in students, and the limitless possibilities to reevaluate in our teaching and learning process to capitalize on the potential of the knowledge era. However, the flip side of that coin is revealed when we consider that some skills will be lost as a direct consequence of the simple fact that this generation doesn't need them. Even as we hail the benefits of having access to unprecedented amounts of information, we must also face reality and contend with the risks that are intrinsic to any period of growth and change.

Content

The first obvious drawback of having a major highway run straight through your living room that can take your children anywhere they like is the fact that, despite our best attempts at developing adult-controlled software that screens and/or blocks Web sites, our students can potentially access content that can be harmful, biased, or erroneous.

This is clearly one of the most difficult risks to address, but denying its reality is futile, and as much as we might try to artificially keep the Internet away from our schools and classrooms, as time goes by, access will become increasingly easier and faster.

Even though it is a tall order, the only self-sustainable way to contend with this worrisome reality is not to try to isolate our children and students in an artificial bubble, but rather to work, from a very early age, at helping our students develop a solid tool set for spotting sites that are erroneous or biased, and to gradually fine-tune an "online intuition" that should accompany them for life.

Harmful content is, of course, a different ball game altogether, and it is a new and dangerous reality of these times that there are Internet shortcuts to sites that children and young people should not be exposed to at all. On the Internet, as in real life, dealing with this aspect of a child's education is a role that families cannot completely delegate, and that takes many hours of dedication, energy, and genuine love. Most ramifications of the 21st-century challenge are open ended. From this risk in particular, we can run but we cannot hide. Harmful Internet content could prove to be a significant factor in the molding of a child's personality.

Imagination

We love to tell our students that in our time, with no cable TV or Internet, we really had fun by playing in imaginary worlds, that we immersed ourselves in fantastic adventures with the sole aid of everyday utensils, and how despite their world full of technology and 3D images, they are missing out big-time when it comes to play.

But deep down, we know that our bravado does not ring true, and that we would give anything to be children again and be able to play with their state-of-the-art gaming consoles and other technological marvels that almost magically transport the younger generation into dreamlike possibilities, of which we have seen a mere glimpse in terms of future development.

But there is an element of truth in our claims, in that children no longer need to imagine much of anything, since, increasingly, software and games deliver the realization of just about any play scenario in real time and with improved graphics capabilities. The definitive coming-of-age of virtual reality also promises to extend the materialization of fantasy to the next level.

Transcending the falsely romantic notion of fighting pirates with a broomstick, the rudimentary nature of our playtime did indeed catalyze the development of our ability to imagine, still an extremely relevant skill in the knowledge era, in which innovation and creativity are unequivocally valued as prime commodities.

Without getting into a technical discussion about the antecedents to the development of certain valuable mental skills, imagining—projecting a sequence of events and possibilities in a hypothetical realm—constitutes the basis for any creative process, so there is a definite risk that children's lack of need to create these mental images may result in a stifled capacity for imagination.

We cannot expect profit-driven companies to generate ways to compensate for this loss automatically, and the responsibility for addressing this issue falls once more on the school system. A new curriculum for the 21st century must acknowledge that imagination is, indeed, an endangered species, and must explicitly and progressively include teaching and learning activities, projects, and assessments that encourage students to develop their capacity to imagine. These strategies must be of value in the curriculum; there is a need for an "imagination pedagogy" to evolve in the near future.

For this and several of the other proposed changes to create a "new-school" curriculum, even a superficial feasibility analysis reveals that some of the old sacrosanct structures of schools do not lend themselves to implementation. We cannot, for example, think of imagination as a subject to be taken alongside math and geography, but rather as one of many trans-curricular skills that will gradually become the nucleus of the curriculum objectives in a school, with the subjects acting as catalysts to the teaching of the skills and not the other way around as per the current model.

Reinventing the Wheel and Creativity

At a time of overabundance of knowledge, it can seem like almost everything has already been invented. Whenever we set out to do anything, we think, implicitly or explicitly, "Let's not reinvent the wheel." Regardless of whether we are looking for a dinner recipe or how to build a homemade solar panel, almost anything can be found online.

The increased power and lower costs of miniaturized devices, 3G Internet delivered through cell phone networks, and the advance of

Wi-Fi coverage allow us to be connected to the Web constantly and almost everywhere. But although we enjoy this era of blissful abundance, never ever having to create anything from scratch or with limited access to external help means that there is a risk that our creativity is being stifled. We can already see in the younger generation a lack of resourcefulness when confronted with certain types of problems that involve finding answers based on estimations and evaluations.

Many of our everyday interactions require us to make judgments and take into account the circumstances to find the right answers. These are things we do automatically. But the excessive dependence on outside resources from a very early age may result in a stifled capacity in this area. Many of the skills that we take for granted that have to do with decision making are built upon being able to make decisions based on our own internal repository of facts, and entrepreneurialism is based upon creative drive—the ability to start something that did not exist before by projecting it in our minds.

Safeguarding and conserving this skill will be the responsibility of schools. The curriculum should include, for example, regular exercises in which students operate in "survival mode," a sort of intellectual boot camp where they will have to solve problems based on their own estimations (also helping to develop the capacity to estimate basic measurements) and without access to the Internet or other external resources. Presenting problems that need to be solved "as is" as a systematically planned exercise in different curricular areas is a good way to try to preserve students' capacity for invention to a certain extent, and it should form part of the new core curriculum, the set of tools in the box that students must graduate with and that subject areas should serve through choosing to teach the content best suited to teaching those skills.

Planning

Albeit to a lesser extent in terms of importance, another casualty of these postmodern times is planning. We live in the just-in-time era, in which the last-minute plan is the norm, and the flexibility and dynamism of the online world allows for real-time decisions both in our social lives and in the workplace. Young people text each other only a few minutes before deciding on that night's outing, so they have no need to regularly exercise the skill to plan ahead. This is even becoming the norm in the business environment.

The ability to plan is essential to the successful and timely completion of more complex projects and endeavors, and once more, schools are called to come to the rescue. Teaching students how to plan and incorporating activities that require systematic planning should be regular features of a 21st-century curriculum.

Paradoxically, we seem to have acquired some of these negative 21st-century traits ourselves, as evidenced in our own shortcomings in planning to incorporate 21st-century curricula elements in our schools. Maybe this issue is the one that educational administrators and leaders should tackle first—we must relearn effective planning skills ourselves before trying to teach them to our students.

What the Internet is Doing to Our Brains

As we progressively become more immersed in Internet-rich lives, we will gradually be able to evaluate what the effect of that prolonged exposure to such stimuli will be, especially in terms of our thinking patterns.

It is almost commonsensical that the younger generation, the one that we are teaching, and the ones that we will be educating in the future, will be profoundly affected by growing up in a completely different world, and, in particular, by the hours spent on the Internet from a very early age. Neurocognitive researchers are slowly gaining more solid ground on scientifically analyzing the influence of the Internet on the development of mental skills and processes, and the impact of "early Internet stimulation."

The book *The Shallows: What the Internet Is Doing to Our Brains*, by Nicholas Carr, provides a fascinating first glimpse into some of the specific studies being conducted in the area. Not surprisingly, findings point to the development of new mental capabilities in children, and, in line with other similar studies, that neuroplasticity continues until well into adulthood. The following paragraph from the book serves to illustrate very explicitly the challenge that lays ahead, and constitutes an apt final reflection to underscore the need to completely reassess the curriculum:

> In a 2005 interview, Michael Merzenich ruminated on the Internet's power to cause not just modest alterations but fundamental changes in our mental makeup. Noting that "our brain is modified on a substantial scale, physically and functionally, each time we learn a new skill or develop a new ability," he described the Net as the latest in a series of "modern cultural specializations" that "contemporary humans can spend millions of 'practice' events at [and that] the average human a thousand years ago had absolutely no exposure to." He concluded that "our brains are massively remodeled by this exposure." He returned to this theme in a post on his blog in 2008, resorting to capital letters to emphasize his points. "When culture drives changes in the ways that we engage our brains, it creates DIFFERENT brains," he wrote, noting that our minds "strengthen specific heavily-exercised processes." While acknowledging that it's now hard to imagine living without the Internet and online tools like the Google search engine, he stressed that "THEIR HEAVY USE HAS NEUROLOGICAL CONSEQUENCES."

CHAPTER THREE

The 21st-Century Classroom

THROUGHOUT ALL DISCUSSIONS that have to do with the 21st-century educational scenario, there is an underlying axiom that is not even discussed. We take it for granted that whenever we teachers get it right—that is, whenever we manage to implement a full-fledged 21st-century pedagogy—our students will spring at the opportunity and seamlessly translate their social and everyday experience with technology into the realm of learning in a formal context.

However, some initial experiences seem to indicate that this transition on the part of the students is not as easy as it would appear. Upon reflection, this makes sense, since students, especially older students, have grown up within the old school, so it is not surprising that they have difficulties breaking out of the mold of traditional teaching and learning. Part of the blame, of course, lies in the fact that attempts at dabbling in a 21st-century curriculum are isolated efforts by pioneer teachers, and students are torn between the prevalent traditional methods and these islands of innovative practice.

THE TEXTBOOK VERSUS OPEN-SOURCE CONTENT

Students' initial reaction when confronted with sources that originate in the rich Internet medium and that know no boundaries is confusion. One might suppose that they would immediately warm to receiving instruction from YouTube video lectures and other similar sources, but, surprisingly, many students are at a loss when it comes to learning from such media. As a matter of fact, they clamor for the textbook and more self-enclosed units of learning that do not involve having to wade through large amounts of information.

There are various reasons for this reluctance on students' part. To start with, they have developed deeply ingrained study habits that rely on being spoon-fed all the material needed for the evaluation, not more, not less, and teachers explicitly stating what will be on the test. Discerning what is relevant amidst extensive amounts of data is simply a skill they have not acquired. Their own consumption of multimedia-related material is indiscriminate in terms of importance and relevance, and never before have they faced the daunting task of trying to isolate what is of value.

Studying from multimedia sources also requires different note-taking skills. Highlighting of important points and other learning aids are built into the formatting and layout of textbooks, whereas listening to an online video or documentary and, for example, taking notes or jotting down links for future reference is a study skill that students do not possess and that must be taught as a prerequisite to moving from teacher-moderated content into the limitless world of the Internet.

At the end of the road, when asked whether they prefer to study from textbooks or be guided to the much more ample spectrum of online information, students say that they prefer the textbook for subjects that they consider of little use or unattractive, but in the case of topics that are of more interest to them, they will gladly invest the time and effort needed to break out of the pedagogy of poverty.

DISTRACTIONS

If the 21st-century classroom is to mirror reality and prepare students in a rich and relevant context for life outside of school, it must account for the issue of multiple Web-originated sources of distraction.

Every teacher who has set foot in a computer room is all too familiar with the virtually futile (no pun intended) effort to prevent students from chatting, checking their e-mail, fiddling with Facebook and listening to or half watching a YouTube video while working on the task at hand. Yes, there are server tools that allow teachers to block these distracting and, in some cases, potentially harmful sites, but the question of whether students will ever learn to determine the relevance and authenticity of information will be unanswered if we do so, as will the question of how well students can deal with distractions.

One of the most easily discernible mental traits of this generation of students is their ability to multitask (or at least they seem to multitask; I will leave it to the experts to determine whether the mind can really multitask or, like a computer operating system, just allocate chunks of time of the mental processor to a series of tasks). Often, this ability results in students being accused of being unable to concentrate and having short attention spans.

An unspoken commandment in most educational settings is "you shall do only one thing at a time," and, granted, the tendency on the part of the students to multitask is not focused on the educational objective of the day but on more fun and irrelevant Internet-based activities. However, should we create an artificial environment cleansed of these potential sources of distraction, or embrace them as part of the current scenario and teach our students how to manage their mental processes in such a way that they can be productive in a real-life atmosphere? What is the use of forcing students to operate in a "clean room" when, as soon as the bell rings and they leave school, they will be exposed to all sorts of distracting stimuli?

That question leads us to a simpler form of mental simultaneity— listening to music, the radio, or TV while you work. Some people need to work in the most absolute silence, and any kind of sound disrupts their concentration, while others, myself included, function better with some background support in the form of music or easy talk. In the Internet realm, there can, in some cases, be increased productivity when users switch between different tasks, some of them relevant and some just fun or distracting. This allows the worker to take short breaks from the efforts required to accomplish the task at hand, or simply to concentrate their energy into shorter and more intense bursts.

In a way, YouTube, Facebook, and the like have materialized, albeit virtually, the ageless habit of daydreaming that has always been indulged in by students listening to lectures and that is secretly treasured in less evident manifestations in the workplace, or at home.

As with most of the challenges emanating from the 21st-century scenario, there is no easy answer, and only through the sharing of experiences, research, and classroom implementation of a Web-enabled environment will we learn more about what the best solution is, for each particular school and district.

MULTIMEDIA EXPRESSION

The students that are now in school have predominantly grown up in the multimedia era, and they have consumed much more in terms of images, sounds, and videos than written text. One might suppose, then, that both studying and demonstrating their proficiency at skills and content using the multimedia language would be a natural extension of their everyday experience.

However, with some exceptions, students who are charged with producing PowerPoint presentations or creating videos tend to resort to slides that are full of text and videos that consist of lengthy and boring interviews.

Without analyzing the learning process itself, it seems that due to the ease with which multimedia is consumed, because of the medium's directness in terms of images, sounds, and videos that hardly need any decoding, it does not trigger an abstraction process that leads to comprehension, and therefore does not provide insight into the inverse process of becoming a producer of that medium. This characteristic of multimedia is what has relegated it to a second-class medium in the eyes of educators, since the consumption of it requires practically no effort whatsoever on the part of the viewer.

What clearly emerges, as we have touched upon before, is the need to teach "video comprehension," so as to become intelligent consumers of the media, and also to explicitly teach the tools and techniques needed to produce start-of-the-art multimedia presentations, as well as principles of graphic design, so as to channel expression through the new media.

USING THE INTERNET TO STUDY

Another salient characteristic of the 21st-century classroom is the extensive use of the Internet for study purposes. What teachers often find when prompting their students to go to the Web to utilize some of those limitless resources for formal study is that students have almost a psychological block that prevents them from applying their fully developed instinctive techniques for browsing and interacting to the formal realm of education.

Students themselves complain about how difficult and counterintuitive it is for them to turn to the Internet as a learning aid, and that is not completely surprising, since from their earliest childhood, kids turned to the Internet almost exclusively for playing and social interactions. Any learning that might take place is embedded in fun or otherwise attractive activities.

As we progressively start to implement these 21st-century pedagogy attempts, we will probably conclude that some of the new mental processes and different neuronal wiring that experts refer to as byproducts of growing up amidst the technological stimuli of our times come hand-in-hand with some deep conceptions about what these tools can be used for. Unfortunately, the educational system's lag in riding the Internet wave means that we will have to build tailor-made educational activities that utilize the Internet into the curriculum from a very early age, so as to disable this block and allow students to associate Internet use with learning. That battle has not yet been lost with older students. The brain is highly plastic, especially in younger people—our students will surely have less "mind stiffness" than we do. But it will entail greater and more sustained efforts on the part of pedagogues to find the best ways to entice older students to use the Internet for learning purposes.

RELEVANT USE OF TECHNOLOGY

In our quest to introduce technology into the 21st-century classroom, we must make sure that the utilization of computers and other technology goes beyond cosmetic use; we must make sure our use is relevant, and not just for the sake of turning on the expensive equipment that the administration has invested in.

Most notorious in this category is the "PowerPoint blackboard," on which teachers type what they would otherwise write on the board in almost entirely text-based presentations that occasionally feature a picture or two so as to qualify for multimedia status. As commendable as this effort is, it barely scratches the surface of what an Internet-enabled computer can do in the classroom, and is quickly discerned by students for what it is, a half-hearted translation of the old model using new tools.

Another, more dangerous, example is computer-based testing. With varying degrees of sophistication, this practice features generally multiple-choice tests that students answer on the computer in a computer lab at the same time as all the rest of their peers, in a fixed amount of time, supervised by staff, with intricate security measures that make sure that no amateur cybercriminal will try to surf the Web and obtain answers to the content-based questions on the test. In an overwhelming flaunting of breakthrough technology, onscreen marking allows teachers to grade open-ended questions and record the grades on the fly.

Again, even as we acknowledge the good intentions behind trying to bridge the gap between the old school and the new school, this travesty of 21st-century teaching and learning eventually does more harm than good, because attempting to teach to the old model using the new media makes for an ill-fitted match: implementation problems are the norm, and the high frustration levels on the part of both teachers and students that result are quite detrimental to the cause of 21st-century education.

Relevant use of technology requires breaking away from the mold and incorporating gaming, simulations, diagnostic software, brain-based learning applications, and a myriad of other increasingly available resources that capitalize on the principles of 21st-century education.

But, even more importantly, it calls for a renewed mindset about the teacher's role. When I polled my students on several occasions about which teachers make the best use of technology, I expected initially to learn that the typical profile of a teacher that can incorporate technology effectively was a young, tech-savvy teacher who uses technology extensively in their everyday life. However, with those not uncommon profound insights that young people are capable of developing, they repeatedly answer that the teachers that make true on the promise of educational technology are those that love learning themselves. They mention how those teachers' passion for their subject compels them to search for the best learning resources, and they share their enthusiasm with their students, to everybody's benefit.

As soon as we reflect upon this, it makes sense: the 21st century scenario of infinite knowledge calls for teachers to be colearners with their students, and those who best embody this changed role will be naturally drawn to the exciting possibilities of online information and tech-enabled tools that enhance learning. This is good and bad news at the same time: forget the expensive and extensive training programs that seemingly hold the key to elevating the technology culture and increasing the skills of teachers in order for them to effectively use technology; the real key is that teachers embrace their subjects with passion and that they desire to learn themselves. How to engender this passion in teachers is a tantalizing challenge in itself, but knowing where to aim, even if we still don't know how to shoot, is the first step in getting the job done.

CRITICAL THINKING, THE REFLECTION PROCESS, AND METACOGNITION

Another perennial contender in the 21st-century skills game is metacognition. It means "knowing about knowing," and is used as a general moniker for knowledge about how students develop the higher-order thinking skills that have forever adorned mission statements in schools and districts.

Going beyond content knowledge itself and fostering higher-order capacities seems to be more within reach these days, as a direct consequence of the fact that knowledge is immediately available and, as such, some mental stamina can be redirected to transcend factual recall and the accumulation of information.

Within many of the taxonomies that have been proposed for this category, there is agreement that critical thinking and reflection are the prime targets for initial focus. Navigating through excessive amounts of information requires the development of a healthy skepticism towards accepting anything at face value, and the capacity to elaborate on one's own and to try to make sense of the overwhelming stimuli is a dire need today and in the future.

Of course, like most skills in the 21st-century framework, there is a great abyss between what we want and the creation of a related functional pedagogy. Some very valuable research has broken down some of the mental skills that comprise critical thinking as a way to specifically address the teaching of each component skill. Reflection is regarded as more of an empirical process, with some clearly relevant surrounding cultural connotations that call out for different approaches depending on the community.

And again, we cannot take for granted that students will immediately respond with joy and success to our attempts to make them indulge in reflection and critical thinking. In order to engage students in meaningful and genuine reflections and other higher-order thinking skills exercises, they have to be trained to do so, and must develop the skills as they would any other capacity that we teach them at school. Initially, since students are not really used to being asked by adults to reflect, criticize, and analyze, they resort to political correctness and easily fall into the cliché of responding by saying what they think the teacher wants to hear. This is seen to an even greater degree if they are asked to express their opinions in writing. So much so that researchers are currently using digital portfolios—handheld devices that allow students to record audio snippets of no more than 20 seconds repeatedly through the task—based on the fact that the short duration of the audio clip allows for greater spontaneity than a carefully construed discourse in front of their peers.

There is, of course, also an element of trust in the process—students will initially be reluctant to be candid about their views, and reticent when they are asked to criticize, until the adult in charge shows them that there are no hidden intentions.

As with most traits that we want to elicit in our students, there is no better preparation for teaching a trait than exercising it ourselves. But, in general, staff meetings are not the epitome of free expression and critical thinking. It would be a good idea for principals and administrators to incorporate moments of reflection and critical thinking into the staff meetings, so that teachers can try it firsthand and see what it feels like to develop the habit of reflection and the building of trust. Incorporating reflection and critical thinking into staff meetings will not only be beneficial to the teaching of these skills to students, but it also constitutes a powerful implicit message about what is acceptable in that environment, and thus will improve the meetings themselves. As we all know, the things that are left unsaid at staff meetings are often far more powerful than those that are addressed openly.

UNCONVENTIONAL ASSESSMENTS

Despite being the hottest topic in education these days, formative assessment in its multiple incarnations (assessment for learning being the most notable) is still far from being a palpable reality in most classrooms. A 21st-century curriculum clearly needs to go beyond the largely sit-down, written, factual-recall, one-chance test that still largely prevails in school systems.

However, when the rubber meets the road and educators start to try out innovative approaches to assessment, like assessment through gaming, letting students write their own assessments, or writing assessments that target higher-order skills, students initially withhold judgment until they see that it is for real, and in some cases they have trouble adjusting to new forms of evaluation.

Use of gaming-based assessments may result in a simple rubric that requires students to advance to higher stages or score a certain number of points that correlate to the grade obtained. Stories from the classroom indicate that students understand clearly what is expected of them, but on some occasions still find it difficult to relate work with play. As with many other manifestations of 21st-century learning that seemingly invade the social/personal realm, initial reactions are mixed, and there seems to be an understandable reluctance among students to let school into their personal lives. For so long, there has been such a marked dichotomy between work and play that any attempts by schools to break into "fun space" are counterintuitive and are met with skepticism.

There are also students who are not very much into video games, and in the classroom, they seem to feel intimidated by the self-proclaimed game wizards, who find it easier to translate their gaming experience into what is required.

The heavily grade-weighted academic culture undermines efforts to stray away from conventional assessment. Being flexible about grades, or allowing students to resubmit their work until it is done properly, also breaks deeply ingrained conceptions of the rules of the game. When I was explaining to my junior year students that, until the end of the grading period, they would be able to redo their e-mail-submitted assignments based on my corrections and observations until they got it right, somebody interjected incredulously, "Then we are all going to get good grades!" as if this constituted an almost blasphemous scenario.

Clearly defined rubrics are the name of the game when you are straying from conventional end-of-unit written tests, and students generally respond quite well when expectations are explicitly outlined. In this case, since many teachers are already effectively utilizing rubrics and using assessment methods other than the written test, it is a matter of doing more, rather than of innovating.

Students also find it difficult to design their own assessment instruments and rubrics, even when properly coached and given precise directions, for the simple reason that they have been passively on the receiving end of evaluations for their entire school lives. For students to be able to be active and not passive in their role in classroom assessment, this is a skill that must be slowly and meticulously taught throughout the lower grades, so that, when it counts, they are ready to tackle it in more complex and meaningful environments.

CONVERTING THE TEACHER ROLE

A key component of any 21st-century classroom is the profound conversion of the teacher from being the "sage on the stage" to becoming a colearner with the students. The difficulty is not just that teachers are used to lecturing and being at the center of the classroom. In a great proportion of cases, educators currently in the profession have chosen it because they love being able to actively share their knowledge, so this targeted shift gnaws at the vocational calling of teachers.

In an ideal 21st-century scenario, teachers would lecture minimally, help students in obtaining publicly available resources, assist them in distinguishing what is relevant, and guide them in assessing whether the skills and knowledge at stake have been acquired, with the ultimate goal of fostering independent lifelong learning.

The indicator of the teacher's success would be, paradoxically, to reach the point where the teacher's role becomes superfluous. When some of my own attempts at using this model of instruction have gone well and, towards the end of the school year, my students have been ready to plan their own learning and continue on their own, I have had an eerie feeling walking through the classroom, resisting the temptation to peer over their shoulders, and being utterly miserable about not being needed to offer help or explain something in the old way. Even though I was a victim of my own success, I could not rid myself of that feeling of futility, until, finding myself with extra time on my hands, I started using it to give students individualized feedback on their assignments, and enjoying the one-to-one personalized interactions that customization in education calls for and that seem unattainable in a real-life classroom scenario. Thus, following this model allowed me to effectively close the circle.

A Tough Class

Pioneer efforts in implementing a 21st-century curriculum serve as eye-openers; they bring to light the many factors that transcend the mere change in pedagogy. To start with, there is the issue of expected outcomes. From state standards all the way down, our hyper-rigid content-based and, to a lesser extent, skills-based expectations are general and absolute, and, as such, loom as indicators of teachers' own success or failure.

For the teacher to relinquish control of the learning in the classroom is intrinsically risky, in that students may not reach these desired markers. As long as there are such fixed external constraints, it takes almost suicidal courage for teachers to embrace the new school model. Before we ask our teachers to take this profound leap of faith (which is akin to the famous movie scene in which Indiana Jones steps into an abyss in the certainty that the bridge will, and eventually does, materialize beneath his feet) we need to turn our schools and districts into places that encourage people to take risks. It boils down to the seemingly contradictory concept of safe risk: if we set goals that are based on the process itself, then the risk dissolves because, even in a worst-case scenario, students will have progressed towards habits of independent learning.

Of course, there is a balancing act to be played to ensure that the acceptable threshold of skills and knowledge is achieved, but the questions about what makes up this essential core of content and skills are not even being asked at present.

And then, there are the students. We must dispel the naïve notion that our students will eagerly embrace a 21st-century pedagogy whenever we manage to get it right, and will eagerly apply their digital sixth sense to formal learning. The new method of learning will probably take less time and be more rewarding, but, like anything else we teach in school, digital learning skills will have to be cultivated and taught systematically and progressively from a very early age.

Donald Scott, a retired NASA educator and wise teacher extraordinaire, brought to my attention a scene in a movie that depicts this with painful clarity. The movie, called *L'Ecole Buisonniere* (literally translated as "the bush school"), is a 1948 classic film set in a school where an old school master is replaced by an energetic, idealistic young teacher shocked at the outdated methods in place. Students under the charge of the old school master are subjected to rigorous discipline, and, amongst other anachronistic classroom rules, have to sit with their arms folded throughout the entire lesson. When the young teacher gets to teach his first lesson, he begins by asking the students to unfold their arms. He is met by dumbfounded looks and no attempt to do as he says. He insists that it is all right and they may, indeed, unfold their arms. As they hesitantly do so, the movie shows one of the students saying to a classmate, "This is really going to be a tough class!"

CHAPTER FOUR

The Educators
of the Future

IF ANYTHING, the 21st-century challenge is all about externals. The
promise of infinitely abundant knowledge and the bright lights of multimedia offerings lure us out into the cyber universe to explore new
sources for learning. Social networks and communications software have
shortened distances and broken down barriers, allowing people of all ages
and from all parts of the world to go beyond the passive spectator role
into interacting with their counterparts from widely diverse cultures.

And yet, almost paradoxically, this outward-bound challenge only
starts to make sense when grounded in a renewed awareness of the
importance of the personal dimension in the teaching and learning
process. The multiplicity of stimuli that can be disturbing, the lack of
safe and well-defined inroads to success, the breathtaking pace of
changes in society that provoke anguish, and the general feeling of
uncertainty that is almost intrinsic to the 21st century all add up to an
assembled puzzle that does not seem to be complete.

THE MISSING PIECE IN THE PUZZLE

The elusive missing piece in the 21st-century skills puzzle points
inward. As we have seen, one of the main drivers in the badly needed
new pedagogy has to do with the conversion of the teacher away from
a center-of-the-classroom role into the role of facilitator and mentor.
This is not just a change in the job description. Not being indispensably
linked to students' learning, and focusing more on the learner than the
teacher, entails a profound change in mindset.

For many teachers, the most rewarding moments are synonymous with passing on knowledge, either through a brilliant lecture or through personal interaction with students. A classical question in job interviews is about a particularly good lesson that the teacher has recently taught, and I have yet to hear an answer that refers to how a great lesson was planned in which students managed to learn on their own, or to develop habits of independent learning.

It needs to be acknowledged that the change required is not merely in the tasks to be performed, but rather in the underlying mindset that prevails in most teachers. In this context, the transition towards a more learner-centered model necessitates more than a new pedagogy; it requires a profound transformation in the general culture and ethos of schools.

PREPARING TEACHERS
FOR THE 21ST CENTURY

Professional development efforts at schools are invariably grounded on technique, teaching strategies and other identifiable specific attempts at revising the way we teach and the way we learn. Countless new pedagogical developments promise to deliver self-contained universal answers to the challenges faced by educators. Somehow, despite the many advances and new theories, there seems to be a pervasive feeling of perpetually falling short, of never really being able to keep abreast of changes.

This is partly due to the denial by administrators and policy makers of the personal dimension of educators. The academic environment has always favored a false split between professionalism and the teachers themselves, as if technique and pedagogy could eventually mask the real personalities of teachers, imposing a sort of postmodern sense of detachment that appears to epitomize good performance.

There are almost infinite technical topics that are dealt with in professional development courses, but the person who teaches is never discussed. Informal discussions and whispered conversations are common in teacher lounges or during after-school functions, but schools never occupy themselves with seriously addressing the personal issues associated with education.

The Person Who Teaches

There is a growing trend in many other professions to increasingly deal with the spiritual issues associated with jobs, and to spend time in the work environment contemplating the personal development of employees. Spirituality, in whatever form it can be defined, is being considered a competitive edge in the 21st century. A Web search for books on spirituality in the workplace will yield many results, but most of them will be unrelated to education.

Not surprisingly, the medical profession is one field that has delved far deeper in searching for personal motivation and in helping practitioners deal with the inevitable emotional turmoil associated with illness, loss, and even death. It is somewhat ironic that education, being in the business of improving life, has so systematically overlooked teachers' inner selves and personal growth.

The great Italian sculptor Michelangelo is reported to have said, referring to his work, "I saw the angel in the marble and carved until I set him free." If we accept one of the main underlying assertions of 21st-century education, that each child must learn, then our role as educators, rather than creating to our own self-image, is to try to "uncover the angel in the marble" by attempting to discover the hidden talent in every student. That kind of attitude calls for teacher wholeness, not only in technique, but also in a renewed mindset and approach to a more profound role as mentor and educator.

A time in which the only certainty is change inevitably requires a strengthening of beliefs and convictions. But more importantly, many of the intrinsic challenges associated with the knowledge era and the availability of infinite information are inextricably linked to our inner lives as teachers.

Beyond the self-evident fact that teaching is a profoundly human endeavor, an analysis of some of the salient characteristics of the 21st-century challenge for educators points unequivocally to the need to highlight, emphasize, and, fundamentally, nurture the personal dimension of educators.

Lifelong Learning

As we have emphasized in the previous chapters, the cornerstone of 21st-century education is the materialization of the ageless promise of lifelong learning, achievable through unrestricted horizontal access to information. Embracing this premise situates teachers automatically as colearners with our students, thus exposing our own passion for learning, which in most cases is the essence of our vocational calling. This particular aspect of the new role of teachers unveils the authenticity of our own joy of learning, as well as our capacity to share it with our students, the true trademark of all great teachers.

Student-Centered Learning

The shift towards a learner-centered approach to education (and away from a teacher-centered approach) requires deep selflessness rooted in a clear awareness that serving our students is our primary mission, and an open-heart mindset that tunes in to each child's unique personality and seeks to uncover their capacities. And those capacities might be well hidden behind their standard "student façade," which is sometimes not the most pleasant or rules-compliant persona. Developing a sensitive awareness that remains unalterable in the face of ever-more-complex circumstances is no small task, and can only be achieved by reexamining our motivation for choosing the profession.

Being more mentors than instructors carries another added challenge. Through our teacher-centered model and one-size-fits-all curriculum delivery and assessment, we implicitly teach to our own model of learning. It is almost second nature to teachers to teach to their own self-image. Parker Palmer (1999) vividly portrays this paradoxical contradiction in educators: "There are dynamics in all kinds of institutions that deprive the many of their identity so that a few can enhance their own, as if identity were a zero-sum game, a win-lose situation. Look into a classroom, for example, where an insecure teacher is forcing students to be passive stenographers of the teacher's store of knowledge, leaving the teacher with more sense of selfhood and the vulnerable students with less."

A renewed mindset focused on the learner requires the humbleness to subordinate to each student's learning style and abilities.

Looking back towards our own mentors, the teachers who made a true impact were the ones who revealed themselves beyond their subject matter and dared show themselves as people to their students. They were invariably educators who were not only interested in academic outcomes, but also in their students as people. And, more often than not, they ended up being the most effective teachers in the school.

Complexity

Another defining aspect of the 21st-century paradigm is the staggering exponential growth of available content and information. The 20th-century left-brained sequential analysis approach to leading and learning has already been dismissed as ineffective given the intrinsic complexity of our era. It has been replaced by a more right-brained, holistic view of leadership that highlights the need to develop nonlinear insights that see through the maze, insights that can provide intuitive comprehension transcending mere facts and analyses. Helping the current generation of students acquire these skills entails our own unlearning of deeply ingrained habits that have resulted from teaching and learning practices almost exclusively focused on grading and measuring, and not necessarily on the personal development of our students.

Interpersonal Skills

Collaboration, global awareness, and other new skills brought about by the flat world and advances in telecommunications are bridging gaps, tearing down the four walls of our classrooms, and exposing our young people to other cultures and interactions with their counterparts from all over the world. Even as we celebrate this unique and unprecedented opportunity for tolerance and the establishment of friendly relationships, we can recognize the perils inherent in the overabundance of stimuli that have resulted, such as young people embracing seemingly alien cultures, lacking a well-defined sense of identity, and displaying disorientation.

The mantra of thinking globally and acting locally as the response to globalization leads not only to a process of finding the identity of the local community in a flat world but, even more importantly, to discovering the uniqueness within oneself as a contributing member of the new society, and the means of anchoring oneself amidst turbulent times. This is not a process that can be taught in the same way as methods and procedures for an academic subject, but it must be modeled by teachers who give of themselves and share their own personal journeys of self-discovery.

Changes

Unfortunately, the pain of exclusion in the face of fast-paced changes is not an unfamiliar scenario in education. Schools embracing the latest trend or pedagogy in an all-or-nothing buy-in inevitably leave out teachers whose styles are ill-fitted to that particular school of thought. And even though this approach derives from administrator shortsightedness in glorifying technique at the expense of individuality, the multiplicity of new trends and theories in the field of education are impossibly pervasive and unsettling to most teachers. Finding a sense of balance and preserving self-esteem in turbulent times implies finding that deep inner reserve that is untouched by pain and wounds and that can nurture our love for teaching.

Need to Connect, Express Feelings

A very important objective in providing contexts for teachers to discuss spirituality is that they have the opportunity to share feelings that are deeper than those shared in staff meetings on pedagogy, technique, and good practice. Most schools include amongst their goals the development of a professional learning community. Douglas Reeves, in his book *The Learning Leader: How to Focus School Improvement for Better Results* (2006), has conducted research that demonstrates that teachers learn from their peers more effectively than from any other form of professional learning. But if staff members have created emotional bonds that stem out of sharing some of their deeper feelings, the creation of a community happens more quickly and naturally. Teaching is a deeply human job, and staff retreats invariably show how educators can find common ground in their life stories that allows them to connect almost immediately. These emotional bonds not only cement professional learning communities, but also more often than not result in an improved climate leading to cultural change.

Modeling Behavior

A major factor influencing student behavior is the way that adults treat each other within the school building, and staff activities that appeal to the teachers' inner selves and foster stronger emotional bonds result in stronger relationships amongst faculty, which then filter down to students in the day-to-day life of a school. Students invariably respond best to those teachers that give of themselves and dare to reach out to them beyond the confines of their instruction. In an academic environment that is always skeptical of explicit messages, when school leaders decide to take time during a very busy schedule to work on personal development, it constitutes a very powerful *implicit* (and, as such, effective) message as to what matters at school.

Need for True Institutional Openness

Creating an environment that encourages reflection may result in the realization that there is a need for healing within the organization, and if steps are not then taken to mend those rifts, the whole initiative may be self-defeating. The call for wholeness includes not only the individual, but also the school, and unless there is true commitment to indulge in a parallel process of soul-searching within the school, it makes no sense whatsoever to foster self-reflection amongst teachers.

TOWARDS A DIGITAL RENAISSANCE

Continuing with the puzzle analogy, Ainsley Rose (2010) uses a good metaphor: leaders may not know how to assemble the puzzle themselves, but it is their role to hold the box that shows the completed picture, so that everybody can have a clear view of the vision that will help them to understand where each piece fits.

The human factor may very well be the elusive missing piece that completes the 21st-century education puzzle, but it will still prove to be a complex challenge, and one that in its very essence will remain ongoing. Adding to the technical difficulties, the need to nurture the human dimension as a necessary foundation for all else seems to make the challenge even more insurmountable.

And yet, the very complexity and uncertainty of the challenge can be liberating and provide educators with a unique opportunity: to center our efforts in the intrinsic, deeply human motivation that lies behind lifelong learning to create a sustainable process for a new renaissance. Paradoxically, the technological developments that have spurred this infinite knowledge scenario could very well become a catalyst to a more human society, one that turns the knowledge era from its current status as a technical challenge into an era of true enlightenment. This digital renaissance will see us take advantage of having access to all accumulated human knowledge by matching our augmented collective intelligence with a renewed sense of self that propels us towards reinforcing the human virtues that are associated with the building of a true community. This newly powerful and spiritual collaboration may very well result in solving some of the problems that have plagued the human race since the dawn of society, like hunger, war, and intolerance, and, more recently, depletion of natural resources and overpopulation.

If any real changes are to occur and the dynamic forces of the 21st century are to be channeled in the right direction, it will be up to schools to lead that movement, through how we respond to the challenge of making sense of the new knowledge paradigm. In targeting primarily the deeper intrinsic human drive for learning and for learning to live together, we may find not only the motivation to sustain us through times of fast-paced changes, but also the key that opens up the 21st-century puzzle and renders it solvable.

AUTOBIOGRAPHY OF
A MILLENNIAL TEACHER

I had always loved teaching. When I was in high school, my classmates used to come home in scores for me to try to explain to them some of the most "complicated" subjects, like Physics and Math. In ways that were difficult for me to process consciously at the time, I was starting to derive pleasure from the act of explaining, and my own learning process became more relevant when I had to share that knowledge later with my fellow students.

I majored in Engineering, and started my first formal teaching assignment whilst still in college, back in 1989. My learning curve of classroom management issues and the rookie teacher years was compensated by the thrill I experienced from transmitting my knowledge to my students, and eventually I settled comfortably into being a successful practitioner. I got along well with my students; my classes were reasonably engaging and the standardized test scores coming along well. Being a teacher of technology, I was happy enough to be a privileged witness to the fast-occurring changes in technology and new advances that promised to truly revolutionize teaching.

And then came the Internet. At first, it was not an epiphany moment, and I can still recall how we were still dazzled by multimedia encyclopedias and regarded the advent of e-mail as a great way to communicate, and little else. But gradually things started changing. The first breakthroughs were again, in my career, associated with communications. We started developing globalized projects, primitive by later-day standards, in which our students shared with their counterparts from elsewhere simulations through a web base static interface, or exchanged data measurements through e-mail. Real time was a chat interface.

The tantalizing human dimension of the global network manifested itself strongly from the very onset. We had developed a very crude Internet-based Space Shuttle simulator, and our students conducted 2-hour simulated missions with students from schools in other places. Once, they had to come in late in the evening to account for the time-zone difference in order to do a simulation with some students in

Colorado. This must have been around 1995 or so. Imagine their grumbling when their fellow virtual astronauts did not show up on the other side of the Internet and stood us up for the sim. The following day I received a message from the teacher I had arranged the activity with, apologizing for the act that they had not attended because they were a school that catered to terminally ill children and one of the students had died.

We were taught a harsh lesson at the very dawn of the Net: what mattered much more than the technology itself was the connection, not the network connection, but the human connection enabled by the breathtaking advances in telecommunications.

But the best was yet to come. Initially an insider's secret, then an emerging contender amongst many search engines, Google started taking the world by storm, even as we struggled to discern the ever-more-blurred difference between what was virtual and what was real. CD ROM encyclopedias slowly bowed out to the exponential growth of online content, and, eventually, Google became the default gateway to all accumulated human knowledge.

As a teacher, I made my own gradual journey, attempting to incorporate as much technology as possible in my teaching, and expanding the four walls of my classroom by making use of multimedia elements and Web-based contents to enhance my teaching. But, inasmuch as I was partial to all these innovations and enjoying the newer technologies, being a first-generation geek, even I was aware that the effect was cosmetic. Sure enough, the brighter and flashier accompanying elements probably made my teaching more attractive, but my lessons were still pumped-up versions of their own selves. My incremental attempts at a changed pedagogy were as ineffective as they were lukewarm.

Taking the Leap

As I was given the chance to teach a completely new technology subject at the school to 16- and 17-year-old students, I decided to take a bolder leap. Mostly spurred by what was clearly an inner urge to expose the students to the new technologies, and after many years of going around lecturing about the theory of 21st-century education, I decided to break free from all the old constraints and structure a completely different class, modeled after principles of 21st-century learning. I decided to be my own case study.

So I started, hesitatingly for the first year, to develop a course that would be an entirely 21st-century immersive experience, featuring the following characteristics:

- Completely paperless, all assignments would be posted on blogs or e-mailed to me.
- There would be no lecturing.
- Resources would be posted on a blog from freely available Internet materials.
- Assignments would mostly be collaborative in nature, and a definitive grade would not be assigned until after multiple instances of feedback were given.
- "Tests" would be open-Web, allowing students to consult their notes, summaries, and any other online materials.
- Whenever possible, assignments would consist of creating multimedia presentations, utilizing simulations and games and other nonconventional assessment forms.
- Gradually students would find and share their own resources for a given topic, create their own assessment instruments, and develop related rubrics on their way to acquiring habits of independent learning.
- Within the learning environment as long as the lesson's objectives were met, while doing their assignments, students would be allowed to listen to music, and some digital distracters (i.e., Facebook, Twitter) would be reasonably tolerated.

What was conceived mostly as a gateway to gain proficiency in the use of state-of-the-art tools and technologies turned out to be a profound eye-opener, and a game changer. To start with, it dispelled any notion that I might have had about the students eagerly embracing the

21st-century setting for learning: invariably, every year, they initially found it very difficult to adapt to the new learning environment, which is not surprising, given that their whole pedagogical upbringing and ancestrally fine-tuned reflexes and instincts respond to the older stand-and-deliver, sit-down, written-test model of teaching and learning.

Other conclusions were related to the actual effectiveness of 21st-century pedagogy and the attempts to mirror a real-life scenario. Students were at a loss when learning from multimedia sources, needing to extract the most relevant information from vast amounts of data, and were woefully unaware of their limitations, in general, when producing multimedia themselves.

By far, the best learning experiences occurred when I was able to find some game or simulation that allowed my students to learn concepts in the syllabus seamlessly through the game itself. My grading consisted in reviewing the game log, which included their game history and time spent playing (most students exceed 24 hours of play, which they would never devote to any other formal learning endeavor—note that I am expressly using the phrase "formal learning" as associated to gaming) as well as their accomplishments in the game or simulation. When reflecting upon the learning that had occurred, students invariably responded, despite having acquired greater mastery on the concepts than in any other activity, that they had not learned much, and were aware that they had merely scratched the surface of the topic. It made sense in that, the more we know, the more we are aware of how little we actually know about something.

The Teacher's Suicide Mission

But the most profound changes were associated with my own role, literally, at the front of the class. As I was gradually successful and was able to leave that physical archetypical position and become more of a mentor/facilitator while students researched their topics and went about their assigned tasks independently, embodying these long sought after traits of lifelong learning, I could not help but feeling a little uneasy. Despite having spurred this change in the normal pedagogy and being a die-hard believer in the benefits of the 21st-century model, I had to resist the urge to peer over students' shoulders or interrupt them to offer a brief explanation to the whole class. My deeply ingrained teacher instincts were rebelling at the seeming futility of my role, and I understood, the first year that I started this experiment, what a profound leap of faith we are asking our teachers to take when we seek that they abandon their center-stage role and stay away from the lure of lecturing.

Of course, having quite some time on my hands during lessons, I reverted to using that time to call students one on one and give them personalized feedback on their assignments, as well as enjoy more leisurely conversations about their progress in the class, thus going full circle and fulfilling, in a small measure, the promise of 21st-century education of reaching out to each learner's individual talents and strengths.

A Learner Reborn

Following this symbolic suicide of the teacher in me, came a more gradual, but not less dramatic, realization: as I relinquished control and embraced a pedagogy shifted towards the learning end of the teaching and learning process, I could shamelessly become a colearner with my students, and rediscovered my vocation more clearly. After a considerable deal of soul-searching, I was able to transcend my somewhat egotistical desire to explain and share my knowledge with my students to rekindle my own vocation as a learner, and to understand, thankfully, that my love of education was really love of learning.

I am now convinced that I am most effective as a teacher when I can share the joy of learning with my students. As a young teacher I knew quite well that one of the capital sins of teaching was to try to talk your way out of the dreaded moment when a student asks a question and you don't know the answer, and that the teacher should truthfully be able to confess, "I don't know." Now we should answer, "I don't know, but let's go and Google that immediately."

CHAPTER FIVE

Technology for the Future

TECHNOLOGY HAS BEEN ON THE VERGE of revolutionizing education for at least the last 25 years, ever since personal computers became widely accessible. However, despite the best intentions of decision makers and multimillion-dollar budget allocations for technology, the promise of technology-rich classrooms that enhance the teaching and learning process has gone largely unfulfilled. This failure to effectively capitalize on the breathtaking advances in technology that dramatically changed the way we live, work, and communicate has resulted in a well-justified skepticism on the part of educators with regard to any new developments or strategies that target the introduction of technology to the classroom.

And even though there are abundant papers and scholarly reflections on the reasons behind this seemingly incomprehensible lag in the adoption of technology by educators, I have found that the best insight into the nature of this paradox comes from the students themselves.

As previously mentioned, students are quick to discern cosmetic use of technology by teachers and identify that the real relevant use of technology is inextricably linked to the learning process. One of the reasons that younger people, particularly in the school context, are less resistant to change is not only because they are more plastic and not so enamored of old ways, but also that their primary role in life is to learn. The only real way to truly embrace change is to see it as an opportunity for learning. The learners will ultimately inherit the earth in times of great change, and this is truer than ever with regard to technology.

This often unacknowledged fundamental tenet of technology in education—that technology is much more about learning than teaching—lies at the heart of the unsuccessful track record of technology implementation in schools.

Most efforts so far have largely targeted technology as a tool for the teacher, and even though tools and software that enhance teaching are powerful aids in creating a more stimulating and enriching classroom environment, the real breakthrough should increasingly target the learning end of the teaching and learning process.

TECHNOLOGY AS A CATALYST FOR LIFELONG LEARNING

Throughout this book I have stressed the fact that the fundamental premise of 21st-century education is the real possibility of learning for life, and that a new pedagogy should target lifelong learning as its overarching goal. I have also repeatedly called out for the need to develop a new teacher mindset, one that converts their role from teaching to becoming colearners with students.

Technology can be the prime catalyst to help produce these changes. If technology is thought of as a tool for the learning community, it becomes a much more natural fit for the classroom. When teachers no longer regard technology as an unsolicited new mandate in their classrooms, but rather as a helpful tool that can add meaning to their mission as educators, there is no longer a dissonance between the existing pedagogy and a technology-enriched one.

THE INTERNET AS A GATEWAY TO INFINITE KNOWLEDGE

The drastic paradigm shift leading into the knowledge era is clearly due to the widespread development of the Internet as the primary medium for accessing knowledge. The inevitable advent of downloadable e-books as replacements for textbooks only serves to reinforce the need to emphasize the use of technology as a conduit for lifelong learning.

The lag in making relevant use of the Internet in the educational process has resulted, especially within the younger generation, in a kind of mental split that disassociates the Internet from formal learning. Young people turn to the Internet for leisure activities, entertainment, and social networking. If we want to get this generation of students who are currently in our classroom to tap into the full potential of the Internet as a gateway for lifelong learning, we need to develop a related pedagogy that trains them from a very early age in the skills they need to deal with the many challenges that are an intrinsic part of the new model.

As I touched upon earlier, we have to help our students acquire the following new skills:

- Dealing with perpetually overabundant data.

- Filtering out erroneous or biased contents.

- Discerning which information is relevant.

- Validating sources in order to determine whether information can be trusted.

- Summarizing vast amounts of information and drawing up key points.

- "Video comprehension" skills that allow students to become intelligent and critical consumers of digital media and proficient decoders of hidden and implicit multimedia messages, as in the "reading between the lines" expression that applies to written text. Perhaps we could call it "seeing between the frames."

Incorporating the teaching of these and other new 21st-century skills as an integral part of the curriculum should be a first priority in any school. The seamless blending in of these skills is not necessarily tied to extensive use of technological resources themselves, and can start from a very early age, for instance, in the design of assessment instruments that incorporate more data than needed.

BUILDING BLOCK FOR COLLABORATION

Another blatant disconnect between education and the real world is the almost obsessive focus on individual work that is the norm at schools. Assessment instruments and various police-like measures are specifically designed to ensure that students can demonstrate their learning individually and without the help of humans or machines. Detractors of the old cooperative learning model have long denounced the method because of the possibility that some of the students in groups or teams might not contribute at the level of their peers and thus "escape" with an undeserved good grade.

Paradoxically, in today's world, regardless of the activity, collaboration is the de facto standard for any productive work. Technology has been a great enabler for this increasing trend, which no doubt will be accentuated in the future. E-mail, social networks, Google Docs, Skype, and an emerging suite of specific applications have provided an easy way to break down even the physical barriers of the workplace and allow people asynchronous and even real-time collaboration in ways that have almost completely eradicated individual work. The extension and generalization of these applications to mobile devices (i.e., Skype is now available on many mobile phone models) promises to extend the possibilities of collaboration even further, providing access on the go to workers in a common project.

The benefits of collaboration are obvious: the increased combined potential of all contributors, the rich exchange of ideas that has long been demonstrated to produce better results, the possibility of integrating various strengths of team members and consequently of providing more opportunities for each team member to find a productive role, and the multiple points of view that are incorporated, to name just a few. The existing pedagogy, however, is completely geared to the individual, and the ability to effectively collaborate must be taught, once again, from a very early age.

The fact that kids are attracted to and engaged by technology, which is their natural medium of communication, makes it easier to bridge this gap, and gradually and increasingly to create opportunities within the curriculum to exercise collaboration. For the sake of accountability, there must be numerous built-in mechanisms that allow teachers to evaluate and track each team member's contribution to the work, as well as specific rubrics that provide ongoing assessment of the development of the project. Techniques that include digital recordings via images and short audio clips of the developmental phases of the project can also help the teacher monitor progress.

Intriguing and exciting possibilities present themselves beyond the classroom. It should be a common feature in schools that students have to engage regularly in developing projects with fellow students from other countries and from other areas of their own country, via projects in which the teams are integrated by shared rubrics, grades, and presentations. When confronted with such challenges, teachers usually fret about what would be the best platform for collaboration, whether to use Skype, Facebook, or e-mail. The best answer is, leave it up to the students. Arrange the teams and give them their objectives; they will usually, on their own, select the most appropriate tool without any problems.

The evolution of computing, increasing network connection speeds, and an increase in cloud computing will continue to open up unprecedented opportunities for sharing knowledge.

Teachers will do a poor job of teaching how to effectively collaborate by means of the new technologies unless they do so themselves. Incorporating this work modality for professional development or other staff-related activities is paramount for teachers to experience firsthand its potential and ease of use, and be able to model it for their students.

GLOBALIZATION

Thomas Friedman probably summarized better than anyone the impact of the globalized, interconnected world in his book *The World is Flat* (2005). This very apt metaphor has captured the general public's imagination and illustrated graphically the concept of a world without frontiers, where barriers have been effectively demolished and the playing field leveled.

However, the overwhelming pressure to become global players, globally competitive, or any of the other well-worn catch phrases that make direct reference to this relatively new phenomenon are focused on the issue of competitiveness. Friedman himself relates the story of how in the old times parents used to say to children that they should finish their food because there were children in Asia starving, and that now parents say children should finish their food so as to grow strong, because there are children in Asia who are hungry … for their jobs. There are endless references in publications about how the United States needs to embrace a more global model so as to retain its preeminent position in the economic and political map of the world, and many of the woes that seem to threaten America's leadership are blamed on the educational system, which is not producing enough graduates, engineers, and PhDs in general.

But, although economic rationale can provide a driver for adjusting programs and making much-needed structural reforms in the curriculum, this extrinsic motivation does very little to appeal to students, or to compel them to reach out and become true citizens of a global interconnected world.

The true wonder of globalization is the opportunity, through technology, to interact in real time with students from all over the world and learn about their cultures, traditions, and lifestyles. Most people enjoy travel, and through videoconferencing, Google Earth, presentations, social networks, and a myriad of other technological tools that nullify long distances, students will experience the joy of relating to their counterparts and, in the process, will learn about tolerance and living with others in a flat world.

In a world in which jobs will no longer be limited to physical location, with outsourcing as an economic phenomenon that is hard to fathom in terms of its economic impact and possible trends, growing up to appreciate, understand, and value other cultures will serve students well—it will help them develop the global mindset that will eventually allow them to find their own niche in the marketplace and ulti-mately, if the educational system is geared in the correct direction, it will help them help the United States to retain its superpower status.

Developing a curricular intervention that fosters globalization is not rocket science. It just requires a deliberate effort to develop class-room activities that involve interactions with students from other coun-tries, and participation in WebQuest projects or any of the multiple opportunities that can be found on the Web for developing global col-laborative projects. Various sites act as repositories of online projects and help teachers to find projects that suit their students based on stu-dent age, subject matter, and other criteria.

PRESENTATIONS

In most high school and international examinations systems, the final requirement for completion of studies often takes the form of a thor-ough and extensive research paper, in which students pick a topic of their choice and, in most cases with the support of a teacher advisor, engage in scholarly research to produce a 4,000-or-more-word written quasi-dissertation that simulates all the features of academic research. I tutor between six and eight students each year for the International Baccalaureate Extended Essay, and I enjoy every minute of it, but I won-der if we are really serving our students well by glorifying the written thesis as the quintessential example of the sum total of students' learn-ing at school.

The benefits of nonfiction writing have long been extolled and are not to be dismissed, but in an era in which very few of us will ever have to write long dissertations, but every person will have to design multi-media presentations and deliver them orally, should we not be shifting our emphasis more towards multimedia and design skills, and the abil-ity to become effective presenters?

Visual literacy is included as a must-teach skill in all 21st-century taxonomies, and all of us who have dabbled in amateur attempts at designing Web sites or posters have painfully experienced how graphic designers who have had specific training in how to convey ideas through images can easily put to shame our long-refined designs with just a few lines and scribbled drawings. It would not be unreasonable to suggest that graphic design, at this time in history, be considered an essential skill.

Classroom practice also seems to point to the fact that contrary to what one would suppose, students do not easily translate their experience as consumers of multimedia material into generating good multimedia content themselves; they often struggle to create dynamic and rich presentations. Schools must supply a systematic training program that targets how to express ideas and messages through multimedia creation.

Acting on this essential premise of 21st-century education requires that school curricula include specific instances in which graphic design is taught from a very early stage in the educational process, and that teachers increasingly include multimedia presentations that include oral delivery as part of ongoing assessment alongside the more frequent forms, such as sit-down written tests.

And if teachers are expected to foster these skills in their students, they must hone these skills themselves, so administrators must provide teachers with similar training (yes, mandatory graphic design courses for teachers) and generate opportunities for teachers to exercise those skills themselves, gradually shifting the focus from the written materials that dominate documentation related to the instructional process in favor of more content-rich multimedia documents.

The Challenger Accident

In his book *Visual Explanations: Images and Quantities, Evidence and Narrative* (1997), Edward Tufte uses the Challenger accident to depict with dramatic clarity how a lack of graphic communication skills may have resulted in a fatal accident that cost the lives of seven astronauts, including school teacher Christa McAuliffe.

On an unusually cold January morning, the O-rings that seal hot gases from the solid rocket boosters, the two rockets that help propel the shuttle into space that can be seen on either side of the big orange external tank, failed to contain combustion gases from the rockets, and that leak, combined with the oxygen and hydrogen that fueled the main engines, resulted in a catastrophic explosion that caused the loss of the orbiter and all crew members.

Morton Thiokol, the firm that manufactured and refurbished the solid rocket boosters for NASA, was aware that these O-rings, which were made of an elastomeric (rubber) compound, had a track record of not sealing properly in low temperatures due to the loss of the elastic properties of the material under very frigid conditions, and warned NASA management the night previous to the launch that a failure might occur. However, when pressed to demonstrate with the data the likelihood of an accident, Morton Thiokol engineers sent a two-dimensional matrix that showed previous failures as disconnected dots. Tufte argues convincingly in his book that other types of graphic representation would have conveyed the risk in a much more compelling way, and thus resulted in a decision to postpone the launch.

HARDWARE IN THE CLASSROOM

Ever since the creation of the personal computer and the subsequent lowering of costs that made computers accessible to households and even classrooms, school administrators have struggled with making the right choices about how to invest their scarce funds in hardware that would deliver on the promise of a technological breakthrough in education.

In the beginning, there was the single computer classroom, then setting up full computer labs and local area networks, and finally overhead projectors, interactive whiteboards, document cameras, clickers, laptops, netbooks, iPads, and other tablet-style computers. More often than not, purchasing new hardware has preceded a rationale for the investment and a related pedagogy to use with it, so teachers found themselves with unexpected and unsolicited machines in their classrooms which had to be used in some way or another in order to justify the expense incurred, and to appear to have a technology-rich classroom.

The success or failure of the introduction of this new hardware is, at best, usually measured in terms of how much it is used by staff in delivering their classes, without a clear idea of how to gauge the effectiveness of the use of the tools vis-à-vis learning objectives. Not infrequently, the promised interactivity degenerates into the teacher lecturing via PowerPoint, with the interactive whiteboard being converted into a glorified and fully lit version of the teacher-centered ages-old blackboard.

When faced with difficult investment decisions, administrators often use a cost-benefit analysis. Cost is easy, but how do we ascertain the benefit side of the equation? To add to the confusion, vendors' aggressive agendas to push their new developments make it hard to discern the best course of action. Exhibit halls at educational conferences are plagued with free T-shirt incentivized vendor demonstrations that extol the virtues of their latest educational hardware.

Even though there is no single right answer, the rule of thumb is to follow the learning. Technology is a great enabler of lifelong learning, so whatever device allows both the students and the teachers to engage in more independent learning and helps to customize the learning experience will probably be a better investment in the long run. Devices that highlight and emphasize the teacher-centered lecturing model are counter to the main premises of 21st-century education.

However, it is more the use of the device than the device itself that determines the effectiveness of the application of technology for learning. Take the interactive whiteboard, for instance. A teacher using it to lecture assisted by a PowerPoint presentation is doing little more than lighting up a "sage on the stage" setup, whereas the use of the whiteboard by the students themselves is more geared to enhancing the learning process. Furthermore, the use of an interactive whiteboard coupled with the increasingly popular personal response systems (clickers) to verify the level of understanding, provide interactivity, or reflect in real time the collective thoughts of the group can really result in a more engaging class and take advantage of the technology to provide students with a meaningful experience that builds upon their knowledge and fosters collaboration.

Laptops undergo similar scrutiny. Software systems are painstakingly designed in order for students to connect to an ad-hoc local area network so that the instructor can propagate centrally emanated wisdom to all student computers simultaneously. But the real benefit of each student having access to a computer is that it can allow each student to engage in independent, self-paced, asynchronous, independent learning as a first step in breaking with the one-size-fits-all, just-in-time model of instruction that still largely prevails.

What will finally be the perfect gadget that will harness the potential of technology for learning? The current minilaptops in all their forms (tablets, netbooks, etc.) are certainly starting to become lightweight, fast, and powerful platforms for learning by every student, and projected improvements in processor speed, storage, and bandwidth promise to continue making them better and more accessible. However, in all envisioned scenarios about education in the 21st century, there is almost always some form of immersive virtual reality learning. Virtual reality has yet to be developed to the extent that it can reach the layman's computer, but we can look forward to the day when realistic three-dimensional virtual reality worlds become available for learning so that students can, together, engage in exploration, inquiry, play, and experimentation in real time. Perhaps by that point, there will be no more papers or books (like this one) that speculate on technology and the future of learning.

PERSONALIZED EDUCATION

One of the essential elements of 21st-century education has to do with acting upon what the best teachers have always known: that each and every child learns differently, has varied abilities, and, as such, will engage in more meaningful learning if the instructional process is tailored as much as possible to that child's learning style.

The one-room schools that preceded the industrialized age did that, to a certain extent and with the means available at the time. Kids of a variety of ages progressed on their own or in small groups, the teachers divided their time and attention to provide what each of them needed, and no lecturing was possible since, by definition, students of varied age levels could not take advantage of whole-group undifferentiated instruction, given their differences in maturity and development.

The advent of the industrial revolution, the extension and generalization of schooling, and the need to teach to certain clearly predetermined standards resulted in our current model of schooling, with classes of between 16 and 30 students on average, all facing the teacher, who is expected to deliver content and skills to all students in the class.

This 21st-century renaissance of catering to each individual's ability as well as fostering collaboration call for a radically different pedagogy, one that allows each child to rise up to his or her full potential, both as an imperative for personal improvement and also in recognition that all talents add to augmented productivity through collaboration. But it would be naïve to think that with the current student-to-teacher ratios educators can be charged with delivering personalized, customized instruction.

Differentiated instruction and other modern-day embodiments of this principle all stumble upon the harsh reality of having to deal with discipline issues, grading, and in general the overworked life of the teacher, thus rendering it almost impossible to think that a single teacher can prepare individualized lesson plans and/or monitor progress of each student in the class.

Here is where technology can come to the rescue. It requires a leap of faith on the part of the teacher, who must abandon the compelling lure of the lecturing podium at the front of the classroom and think more as a mentor/facilitator/coach than as an instructor. Software packages are evolving towards identifying the best possible pathway for learning based on initial diagnostic assessments of the user. Without getting to that extreme, games provide an engaging and interactive platform that enables students to progress at their own rhythm, make mistakes, and customize their learning via the traits and characteristics of their in-game avatars.

As I already mentioned, even though I know from my own personal experience that helping students acquire habits of independent learning allows me to have one-on-one mentoring interactions with those students, it is hard to let go of the control position; it is contrary to our well-honed teacher instincts, especially in an academic culture that is so adverse to risks.

Linear Representation Meets Computer-Generated Graphic Text Analysis

A good example of how technology can help students develop a holistic, across-the-board ability to read through very complex data is Wordle. A free Web-based application (www.wordle.net), Wordle processes any input text and displays the most-used words in a size proportional to the number of occurrences in the text, giving a powerful glimpse of, for example, what themes and issues are important when processing free-response questions to a survey. Albeit lacking in numerical results, Wordle presents multiple displays that represent with great clarity key phrases in complex text and constitutes a great aid in text analysis. This emerging field will undoubtedly add more powerful and versatile applications to the professional high-end text mining and analysis software that is available already, in ways that make them more usable and accessible to the layman user.

GAMING AS A LEARNING TOOL

The infamous line from the evil and abusive Miss Trunchbull, the headmistress in Roald Dahl's children's novel *Matilda*, "If you are having fun, you are not learning," has sadly impregnated the subconscious thinking of many a teacher and administrator in schools. Whenever students are really engaged and, as such, can let themselves act as if they were not in school, interacting with each other, and, possibly, learning in the process, we start thinking that something must be wrong.

And this preconception is never more flagrant than with the use of games for learning. It is hard to explain why serious games and simulations are not used more extensively in the classroom, since games are such a self-evident incarnation of all that is good about 21st-century learning.

Students are engaged, they progress at their own pace, they feel free to make mistakes and try again, they receive immediate feedback, they can customize their learning experience, they are faced with increasingly more difficult challenges as they gain mastery, they naturally consult with their peers face to face or via forums when they are stuck, they collaborate seamlessly in multiplayer games, and, essentially, they have fun.

It may be argued that not enough realistic games are developed for learning, but a simple Web search will yield many more than you think, with more than a few being free of charge or available for a very low cost. In upcoming years, more and better educational games will be developed, and the improvements in graphic capabilities and processor speeds will surely also pave the way for three-dimensional realistic simulations to become more commonplace and available to students and teachers. Virtual reality, as mentioned earlier, with full-body sensors, will also take the gaming/learning experience to a completely new dimension, and it's just a matter of when it will happen, not whether it will happen.

In the meantime, teachers and administrators should start getting ready for the inevitable and try to infuse as many gaming experiences into the curriculum as possible, as well as developing rubrics and other assessment methods that incorporate students' educational gaming achievements into formal learning.

E-BOOKS

One of the questions that I get asked most often when doing presentations is about the presumed demise of textbooks, and whether it is worthwhile to invest in any of the electronic book readers that are flooding the market. Teachers and many in the general public have developed a fondness for books that goes beyond rational or logical analysis, and paper books seem to represent the only remaining bastion of a bygone, "purer" era that preceded the digital revolution. It is as if they were the last stand of civilization in an increasingly schizophrenic world. Stalwart defenders of books postulate that the touch, look, feel, and smell of books will never be replaced by impersonal electronic devices which, to add, in this case, injury to insult, they say also harm the eyes.

Unfortunately for the book romantics, it is not a matter of principle, or even of taste, but of economics. In the same way that reference books, and, in particular, encyclopedias, have pretty much disappeared, mostly due to multimedia capabilities, the advent of the Internet and the high production costs of printed books will result in electronic books eventually replacing their paper counterparts as they become more inexpensive.

As of this writing, e-books, in general, cost somewhat less than paper books, but it is almost inevitable that they will eventually end up costing a small fraction of the price of the "real thing," and then even the die-hard defenders of paper books will have to yield and fire up their devices to read electronically. (I myself am a self-confessed book lover; perhaps some manufacturer of e-book readers will be kind enough to offer devices that come with a paper scent, to appease us!)

The school consequences of the eventual phasing out of textbooks in favor of some electronic form of books are obviously all very positive: students would not be condemned to hauling excessive weights to and from school, teachers would not need to prescribe a single textbook per subject and could instead take advantage of a multitude of sources, multimedia would be added to text, students would be able to take advantage of the features of e-books that help to customize learning, and schools would be able to accrue substantial savings.

In terms of who will win the technology battle, dedicated electronic readers (i.e., Kindle) or smart phones/tablet computers, it is hard to conceive that a single-purpose device will really be sustainable over time, so my instincts tend towards favoring the tablets in the long run, especially if they increase speed and connectivity. However, since the cost of the dedicated readers is lower, and the electronic ink system they use is less tiring for the eyes than any of the current small, general-purpose gadgets, those devices still make sense. However, we may reasonably expect that e-reading, in the future, will be just one more feature of a combined tablet/personal computer/cell phone.

CELL PHONE: FRIEND OR FOE?

The cell phone is regarded as public enemy number one in most schools. These omnipresent and ubiquitous devices, whose capabilities seem to be growing with every minute that goes by, are sneakily used by students in and out of lessons for all conceivable purposes, albeit none that are related to learning.

Schools have policies with varying degrees of strictness concerning the use of cell phones, when they are not banned altogether from the building. And even though their distracting effect cannot be argued against, cell phones also represent a low-cost option for mobile technology that, when appropriately channeled, can result in successful classroom applications.

Most cell phones, for example, now come equipped with cameras, which can be used to photograph and document completion of a project as part of a digital portfolio. Text messages are the standard means of communication amongst young people, and as such can catalyze collaboration. It is also increasingly common for students to be able to access the Internet, send e-mail messages, reproduce videos, and accomplish a long list of other applications with their cell phones, which makes them resemble in some ways those long-sought-after laptops that most schools cannot afford.

Like any tool with great potential, its use determines its effectiveness, and there are many resources on the Web about how to put cell phones to good use in the classroom. Involving students in the development of a consensus policy governing the use of cell phones seems to be the way to go. Their increasing power and speed, as well as the progressively lower costs for the devices and data plans mean it makes sense for schools to try to harness their potential rather than banning them. And banning the phones would mean teaching students in an artificial world.

THE WORLD OF THE FUTURE

If schools are to prepare students for the future, we must take a look at trends that will affect everyday life. Fast-paced technological growth might lead to the materialization of some things that only a few years ago were reserved for the realm of science fiction.

In particular, advances in artificial intelligence, coupled with advances in processing power, have yielded breathtaking results. Project Milo, for example, a next-generation artificial intelligence creature, featured an intelligent boy or girl who could communicate with humans and was able to interact almost seamlessly with them, allowing object transfer, manipulations, and real-time interactions that are almost uncanny. And although Microsoft has recently stated that Milo was only a technological demonstration, it does constitute an initial peek at the direction in which artificial intelligence will inevitably be growing.

Even though they are still in the developmental and prototype phase, advanced humanoid robots are capable of simulating human traits and capabilities to the point that they can pretend to have feelings for the humans they interact with, and even display self-consciousness.

One of these prototypes, Jules the Robot, a creation of Hanson Robotics (www.hansonrobotics.wordpress.com), is seen on several YouTube videos having conversations with humans and would be indistinguishable from a real human, save for the metallic voice and the protruding wires in the back of his head. A particularly telling moment is when Jules is confronted with a baby, and he says to the child, "You might not remember me, but I will never forget you."

Although the emotion in the statement is programmed rather than felt, this seemingly inconsequential exchange really opens up tantalizing possibilities. The underlying technical support for the above statement is simple enough: a retina scanner in the robot stores the image in a database alongside with other relevant information and, many years later, when the robot matches the biometric recognition with that stored in the database, it can easily retrieve from its memory whatever information is necessary to remind the now-grown person about where they met, what was said, what the weather was like, and endless possibilities according to what the robot's programmer chose to store.

The real breakthrough will occur when these humanoids, which can already be programmed to develop simulated feelings, also incorporate system capabilities that increase their knowledge with usage and are trained to detect moods and inflections, and thus can provide their personal users with the best response in any situation: play music, find adequate quotes, and, in sum, develop almost superhuman capacities. It would not be out of the question for humans to become attached to such devices (especially if they are good-looking, as a student of mine pointed out once while we were discussing this issue in class).

Even if the study of human-machine interactions still seems like quite a stretch of the imagination, the emerging field of roboethics deals precisely with that—the study of relations between humans and robots.

How does this relate to schools? As a Web search will readily attest, some pilot experiences with robotic teaching assistants are being made to carry out some of the more mechanical tasks related to instruction. Even if that were not the case, students need to be aware of the advanced capabilities of robots and progressive developments in the field of artificial intelligence, because in the future, advanced robots or software creations will come closer to challenging the distinguishable limit between artificial creations and humans. As unsettling as this may ultimately prove to be, these superhuman robots will be commonplace sometime in the future, and the whole issue of relations, dependence, feelings, and attachments with machines must be dealt with in the open, in order to provide our students with firmer ground in a world of the future that promises to be dramatically different.

Futurist Ray Kurzweil deals with this issue in his book *The Singularity is Near* (2005), a sequel to his previous work *The Age of Spiritual Machines*. This provocative concept of singularity refers to the point in the evolution of machines in which intelligence becomes nonbiological, and humans and machines become one, uniting computational intelligence with our biological capabilities. The singularity may be near, but certainly our collective awareness and understanding of the implications of the developments of super-intelligent machines is still far away. As teachers, we need to educate ourselves about how technological evolution will result in a different world, one that, despite our best intentions to preserve the essence of what we think is important, will create a different, more complex landscape.

CHAPTER SIX

Leading Into the Future

I N AN ACTION THAT HAS TRANSCENDED HISTORICAL FACT to embody one of the boldest metaphors of change, Spanish conquistador Hernán Cortés, on the eve of a deciding battle during his quest to conquer Mexico, assembled his troops and, in plain sight of all of them, burned the ships in his fleet, rendering them effectively unusable and thus conveying a compelling message: there was no turning back—the new world would become their new home, and victory was their only option.

And, even though the circumstances are far less dramatic, leaders in the school setting are facing a similar quandary. The temptation to continue with the old ways—to still hold onto a lifeline to the past— remains too strong for educators. The 21st-century challenge for education really constitutes a new world, with a completely changed underlying knowledge paradigm that requires new solutions, and our natural and justified aversion to bold change in terms of school reform can definitely hinder the change process.

Bringing about changes of the magnitude required is a formidable challenge for educators. Education is probably the most conservative business that exists, and justifiably so, since the subjects of any experiment in reform are the students, whose learning must not be jeopardized. However, and understanding the need for caution, incremental change processes are not always the safest way to go about modifying the status quo, and finding the right equilibrium between a motivating vision for the future and the related implementation model is always an elusive quest.

Much has been written about leadership, both in the pre-Internet era and the current context, and the role of leaders is formidable enough without the added challenge of the change in the rules of the game that results from the new educational model. In the next few sections we will attempt to shed light on the implications of the new paradigm for school leaders and explore some of the drivers for the evolved role of leaders in the 21st century.

LEADERSHIP IN THE 21ST CENTURY

We have already made reference to the idea of adaptive challenges mentioned by Ron Heifetz, challenges that are open ended and complex by nature, that have no easy single solution, and that require lateral and creative thinking to address them. The 21st-century context is one big adaptive challenge, in that fast-paced changes, overwhelming amounts of data, exponential growth of online contents, and other defining characteristics present a dynamic and confusing set of problems for current and future leaders in the school system.

It needs to be understood that, in the same way that the new paradigm calls for a new teacher mindset, the challenge for leaders is similar in its depth. Profound beliefs must be revised in order to rise to the occasion and not be frustrated by the uncertainties and unknowns that are intrinsic to the 21st-century education model. Leaders have to grapple with an ever-changing situation and still be able to lead the way, accepting once and for all that their role increasingly calls for managing complexity rather than controlling it.

A great metaphor of the current times and what leaders are up against is a TV commercial from EDS (now HP Enterprise Services), on building planes up in the air. The video shows workers, engineers, and the crew are assembling and piloting a plane in the air, while the passengers are stoically enduring the chaotic conditions of open-air flight. Some of the workers are swept from the plane and activate their parachutes, and flight attendants pour coffee that is blown around by the wind, while an off-screen voice relates how they love the challenge of building planes up in the air. The commercial is meant as a metaphor for the company's technology services, which the firm performs while their clients are running their business as usual, but it also serves as a good metaphor for the job of school leaders in the 21st century. Educational leaders have to put together a very complex operation while everything is still running, and while the world is still changing.

The lack of standardized predetermined outcomes for success adds a further layer of complexity to the leadership quest, and the prime tenet of 21st-century education, an awareness of the need to nurture each learner's talent, can be extrapolated to staff. The days of a single-minded focus on a few chosen instructional strategies are long gone; in the same way that we seek to peel off the layers of students so that their true self can emerge, it requires a deep conviction to allow, within limits, for teachers to also rise up to their full potential.

THE WAY WE WERE

One of the greatest difficulties faced by this generation, and one that is probably emblematic of 21st-century challenges for all activities, not just education, is that most of what we learned, the mentors we had, and many of the tools in our toolkit are mostly outdated and no longer very useful. Those of us who learned most of the tricks of the trade from practicing administrators of the old paradigm find ourselves woefully unprepared for the needs of the time. Even so, we must embrace the future, because, as was the case for Cortés's army, our ships have been burned and we cannot go back.

To understand the challenges that we face, we must compare the main characteristics of the old style of leadership against the 21st-century scenario.

Analytical

One of the most desired traits in leaders in the 20th century in all fields, not just in the educational arena, was the ability to analyze and break down data and make related decisions. This prevailing underlying framework resulted in matrices, graphs, indicators, and an innumerable list of representations of reality that could be analyzed and interpreted. Juxtaposing that analytical model with the 21st-century environment of infinite data and knowledge immediately reveals a dissonance. The overwhelming amount of data, fast changes, new trends, and dynamic problems require skills in leaders that go beyond the analytical, since it is now impossible to come up with complete or even abstract models for a very complicated reality. Leaders who need to see all the data before making a decision are frequently unsettled by the complexity of the new school, and on occasion are reduced to inaction because of their inability to grasp the whole set of circumstances. I have seen many a team of old-school administrators baffled by the sheer complexity of a problem and unable to commit to a course of action because the outcome is not clear enough.

Linear Model of Accountability

Another big theme in schools is the frequently brandished organizational flowchart that attempts to boil down to geometric relationships the very diverse and intricate nature of school systems. The clear-cut division of roles and responsibilities may have worked very well in the past, but the characteristics of schools themselves and the transient nature of almost everything in the current context underlines the futility of such efforts. Organizations in general and schools in particular have been increasingly likened to organic models, a term that reflects the interweaving links and relationships that exist within them. This discrepancy between the theoretical reporting chain and what really happens is a testament to the intrinsically dynamic environment of schools, and all such considerations are clearly more relevant in the face of an external frame of reference that no longer calls for such a compartmentalized structure in schools. Leaders in the current context, more than ever, need to go beyond organizational flowchart boundaries and be alert and responsive to the dynamic needs of the school.

Hierarchical

Schools have traditionally placed heavy emphasis on hierarchies, and in most schools, power resides at the top levels of leadership. Hierarchies work well within a clearly defined, linear model that can progressively be encompassed by fewer persons of increased capabilities. But the increasing complexity of school processes casts a shadow over a model that places too much weight on few shoulders, and the all-too-frequent cases of school administrator burnout may be an indicator to that effect.

Control-Based

Much of the ideology behind leadership strategies in the old school was geared to exercising effective control—the model used in schools was a sort of translation of the quality control model that was the foundation in most corporate environments. Appraisal systems, accountability frameworks, and other similarly developed instruments that leaders utilized to monitor the status of schools were conceived primarily with that end in mind. Relatively uniform instructional strategies and a more single-minded approach to school improvement resulted in an important part of the administrative role being geared towards controlling the effective implementation of such plans. As we recognize the diversity of talents in our students and staff and move towards a more customized and flexible model of schooling in the 21st century, control is not only less relevant, but also much more difficult to exercise, since the outcomes are not as predictable.

Goals-Oriented

For a great deal of time, goals and objectives have ruled organizational environments, including schools. Administrators, department heads, teachers, and nonteaching staff members have all been subjected to the goals tyrannically and measured against attainment of these objectives. Many staff members would whisper, when out of the earshot of supervisors, that these goals were severely limited in that they usually failed to reflect the whole range of activities that comprised the job or role of the person in question, and usually focused only on improvement factors that very often were more tailored to the needs of the supervisor than those of the employees themselves. However, research suggests that the open-ended and dynamic environment of the 21st century lends itself much more to intrinsic motivation than rewards-oriented goals, as Daniel Pink pointed out in his July 2009 TED Talk on the "Surprising Science of Motivation" (www.ted.com). Goals and their ensuing rewards will never go away altogether, and even within the more unpredictable 21st-century environment, having an ordered set of objectives to comply with can prove useful, but they will surely lose their preeminence and give way to a more dynamic leadership framework that pays more attention to *genuine* motivation than that which stems out of compliance or desire for recompense. The difference between compliance and motivation is, in part, generational. Most educators are from a generation that was brought up to offer blind obedience to authority figures—we did things even if we did not see the purpose. But today's students are not hardwired that way, and will only do something if they think it has meaning.

High-Profile

Great leaders have always been associated, even in the school context, with larger-than-life, super-charismatic personalities that loudly instill their presence in all echelons of school life. The prevailing model, based on clear definitions of what was to be expected at school, resulted in leaders who were able to communicate these expectations unambiguously. Having a high-profile personality was almost a prerequisite for being a leader. In the 21st century, the need for authenticity and the availability of knowledge (about both content and people) to everyone are slowly changing the landscape. What is needed now are leaders who may not be so prominent, but who truly embody the values of the organization.

21ST-CENTURY LEADERS WANTED

An interesting exercise is to try to write an advertisement looking for a 21st-century leader for a school. What traits and desirable characteristics would we seek? Below the "Wanted!" heading we would probably require that candidates have the following characteristics:

Learning Leader

The Learning Leader (2006), the title of an excellent book by Douglas Reeves, is also the first and foremost characteristic we want in a 21st-century school leader—we want that individual to be a learner at heart. If the name of the game is lifelong learning, then, of course, the leaders must be great at this game, or at least enjoy playing it. In an era in which authenticity prevails, educational leaders can't fake it—they must enjoy learning themselves, in ways that are self-evident to all involved. This is not just about being a scholar, or even publishing papers, but rather about having a learning mindset—exuding a genuine joy of learning that permeates the whole school. Leaders must possess this infectious enthusiasm about the latest ideas, trends, and innovations in a way that not only encourages the rest of the people in the organization to embark on the same learning journey, but also conveys an all-important implicit message about embracing change. Learning is clearly the best immunization for the disruptiveness associated with change, and the fast-paced changes that are the norm in the 21st century can only be embraced with a genuine disposition to permanently learn. Eric Hoffer, a social writer and philosopher, is quoted as saying that "in times of change the learners inherit the earth, while the learned find themselves wonderfully equipped to deal with a world that no longer exists."

Visionary

T. E. Lawrence (better known as Lawrence of Arabia) wrote in *The Seven Pillars of Wisdom* (1926), "All men dream: but not equally. Those who dream by night in the dusty recesses of their minds wake in the day to find that it was vanity: but the dreamers of the day are dangerous men, for they may act their dream with open eyes, to make it possible." The current context needs visionary leaders, leaders who, by virtue of their words and their acts, are constant reminders of the vision of the school. Losing sight of the vision is a common malady in organizations and not exclusive to the 21st-century scenario, but in tumultuous times, sustaining motivation through the vision becomes essential to navigating change. This is not only true for schools, and there has been a reassessment of the importance of emphasizing the core values, mission, and vision of organizations throughout everyday life.

Simon Sinek has made a compelling case for the fact that great leaders manage to put the "why" of new strategies first, and remind people of the vision and mission, in his book *Start with Why: How Great Leaders Inspire Everyone to Take Action* (2009). Because so many profound changes are needed, and teachers, students, and families in the school community will be asked to step out of their comfort zone, putting the mission up front becomes more necessary than ever. The role of the leader not only entails sustaining this vision, but also being instrumental in developing a bold vision, one that will inspire people within the school. Since we are in an era of transition, bridging the gap between the old and the new paradigms in education, creating a powerful vision of this new paradigm is an integral part of the role of the leader. Managerial skills and the rest of the abilities that are traditionally required of school leaders will, of course, continue to be necessary, but more importantly, leaders must embody and embrace a courageous vision of the future.

Embodies Values

Twenty-first-century schools need leaders who embody the values in the mission statement of the school or district. It is no longer enough to talk the talk, and there is a gradual trend in leaders in all kinds of organizations to shift from super-charismatic personas to not-so-brash, quieter, more reflective leaders that truly embody organizational values. In his book on how companies are able to sustain excellence, *Good to Great: Why Some Companies Make the Leap ... and Others Don't* (2001), author and management guru Jim Collins states a very strong case for what he has labeled as "Level 5 leaders," that is, leaders who are humble, possess a strong will, have the organizational vision foremost in their goals, and are not necessarily overpowering in their demeanor. In an interview on the management portal management-issues.com, the author summarizes his ideas on Level 5 leadership: "It came down to one essential definition. The central dimension for Level 5 is a leader who is ambitious first and foremost for the cause, for the company, for the work, not for himself or herself; and has an absolutely terrifying iron will to make good on that ambition."

In the school environment, administrators that make a difference are the ones who not only deliver great speeches about school achievements or relate well with the educational establishment, but who really enact the values and the mission of the school itself. Rallying, inspiring, motivating people to change for the greater good, as is required in this moment in history, can only stem out of genuine beliefs.

Principle-Oriented

While 20th-century leaders were primarily goal-oriented, 21st-century leaders must be primarily principle-oriented. Given the ephemeral nature of new fads in the current century, the intrinsic unpredictability, and the exponential changes occurring, leaders must be able to adjust and reassess organizational goals in a very dynamic way. In order to effect midcourse corrections, leaders need to not be so attached to fixed objectives, but rather must operate according to principle, since basic premises and values are unmovable and constitute a good reference point from which to successfully navigate change. An excessive reliance on fixed or very precisely set out objectives can not only lead to increased levels of frustration, but also to misallocation of precious time and energy, the scarcest and most valuable resources in schools.

Embraces Uncertainty with Confidence

There is a wealth of knowledge about change management, but the school environment poses a dire challenge to leaders who will be guiding schools and districts in times of great change, because schools are essentially places where, in the words of Gene Kranz, flight director for the legendary Apollo missions, failure is not an option. For teachers, who are charged with knowing it all, uncertainty has until now been seen as tantamount to weakness, and the same has been true of leaders. But embracing uncertainty, modeling what we can call a "confident uncertainty approach," is important in the new school, for both teachers and leaders. It is especially important for leaders, because implicit messages are very powerful in schools. The general attitude of leaders towards change and uncertainty will cascade down within the organization, and confronting innovation, paradoxes, and change in general with unreserved confidence will inspire teachers to do the same.

Intuitive Decision Maker

Even though it would look bad in a job advertisement and is very difficult to frame in proper terms, the ability to develop a holistic vision of the organization and adhere to it by making intuitive decisions that incorporate complex data about mostly open-ended problems would also be a desirable characteristic of a modern-day leader. The old school's linear analytical model is rendered ineffective by the overwhelming amount of data to process. Leaders must learn to follow their well-honed instincts and jump-start processes, even if the outcomes are not clearly determined. This is not a call for suicidal plunges into unknown initiatives, but the very dynamic and complex nature of school systems in the new paradigm can result in school improvement processes being stifled when administrative teams take too long to decide on initiatives because of the lack of a clearly outlined course of action. The model under which most of us have been trained, of meticulously planning every step along the way, and determining a critical path and carefully evaluated outcomes, can no longer be the norm, especially in processes of school reform that span several years. Ray Kurzweil (2005) is quoted as saying "Measured by the atomic clock, the twenty-first century will contain a hundred years. Measured by how much will happen in the twenty-first century, we will experience twenty thousand current years." Regardless of the exact numeric equivalence, it is certain that several years in the 21st century is the equivalent of at least several decades in the 20th century. Leaders cannot afford to be bogged down by the need to see the whole process unfold in their minds before taking action. Needless to say, finding the right equilibrium between being daring and being reckless is an art in itself, but there is a clear need for leaders to develop a broad holistic vision and base their decisions on that, rather than on meticulously planned initiatives.

Team Builder

The 21st-century leader must generate teams that mostly operate on consensus. The old school's top-down leader that dictated policy to be obediently fulfilled by subordinates is outdated, especially in the context of schools, which are complex environments where it would be absolutely counterproductive to try to enforce compliance with the leader's will. The open-ended and interconnected essence of the 21st-century environment renders all attempts at forceful control useless, and is fertile ground for leaders who endeavor to work through consensus and create teams. The seamless opportunities for collaboration also call for school administrators to truly operate as a team, utilizing the pooled talents of all members to augment the capacities of the administrative team as a whole. In that respect, the use of state-of-the-art technological tools for collaboration should be encouraged, and, even though some decisions will still heavily rely on the always-burdened shoulders of principals, most everything can be worked on collaboratively. An old principle of leadership is that a true leader is one who gets the people under his charge to act according to the leader's (or in the modern scenario, the school's) ideas without even remembering that it was the leader who motivated them. Going back to what Jim Collins defines as one of the key characteristics of the Level 5 leader, and one that seems at first glance counterintuitive—humility—a quote attributed to Harry Truman illustrates this point with decisive clarity: "You can accomplish anything in life, provided that you do not mind who gets the credit."

One of Us

During a presentation that I once attended, the speaker recounted how staff members at a school were sizing up a new principal that had just been introduced to them. They were asking themselves the defining question: "Is the new principal one of us, or one of them?" Having disconnected leaders who seem to lose touch with reality once they are elevated onto their administrative pedestals, and who don't seem to know what is really going on at the classroom level, is probably the main source of discontent and irritation for staff regarding leadership. Paraphrasing Ron Heifetz and Marty Linsky's metaphor of the balcony and the dance floor in *Leadership on the Line: Staying Alive Through the Dangers of Leading* (2002), leaders need to be not only up in the balcony, but also occasionally on the dance floor. Leaders must both immerse themselves in processes and then step out to look at the processes with a bird's-eye view. This has always been a desired trait in leaders, but the dire need for authenticity that is a trademark of the 21st-century scenario emphasizes this even further, and the fact that staff in school are exposed to overwhelming and confusing multiple stimuli requires that leaders not just talk the talk, but that they also walk the walk.

Once I was stuck in a remote holiday spot with a book that had been given to me as a Christmas present. Upon starting to read it, and having no bookstores within a negotiable distance, I was appalled to find that it was a compilation of stories about military strategy which, with all due respect to those who enjoy reading about such things, was completely uninteresting to me. I stuck with it mostly out of boredom, and was rewarded with a story about an African general that the author used to illustrate the mettle of true leaders. This military commander was recounting an operation in which he was trapped by the enemy, and in order to escape with the main body of the army at his command, he had to devise a diversion maneuver that resulted in some of his troops being killed. As he was telling the story, which had taken place many years earlier, the general was openly crying, because he felt for his troops, and was still a soldier at heart. We need to fill our administrative roles, with all their associated intricacies, but we must always feel, act, and think of ourselves as teachers.

APPRAISAL IN THE 21ST CENTURY

A quintessential part of the job of any school leader is evaluating teachers. Perhaps it is because teachers make their living mostly through evaluating students that they have a particular aversion to being assessed, or maybe it is because of today's accountability systems, which can feel like "revenge." Either way, teacher appraisal has become the bête noire of the leadership role in schools.

Reconciling staff and administrators' views on teacher appraisal seems like an almost futile effort. I have participated in more workshops than I care to remember that tried to define or refine teacher appraisal systems, and when teachers and administrators attempt to enumerate the desirable characteristics of the ideal system, most of them are mutually incompatible.

Appraisal must be frequent enough to be genuine, but not constitute an excessive overload for administrators; must be focused on development and professional growth, but must provide a measure of accountability; must be spontaneous, so that teachers do not put on a show, but must not rely exclusively on unannounced observations when an instructor may be caught on a bad day; must not be judgmental, but, on occasion, must be linked to pay; must use rubrics that are thorough so that teachers know what is expected, but must not be rigid so that everybody is not measured by the same standards; must incorporate feedback soon after the observation, but must not be based exclusively upon observations; and so on and so forth.

There is an enormous body of literature, doctrine, and dogma related to teacher appraisal, and numerous frameworks are available for use by administrators. Nonetheless, teacher appraisal is often the number one point of disagreement between school leaders and their staff. It is a game that must be played and endured. In many cases, even the administrators are only halfheartedly going along with the rules of engagement because it is almost intrinsic to the leadership role and is expected by their supervising bodies.

It is interesting to analyze, then, how the new context of the 21st century, with its associated variables, can be a factor in possibly easing some of the tension intrinsic to the teacher appraisal process.

The first thing that comes to mind is how to define proficient teacher performance. The modern realization that education is a customized and personalized business applies to teachers also, and most appraisal frameworks are fundamentally flawed in that they treat all teachers the same; and we all know intuitively that all teachers are not the same. One of the wonderful things about being an educator is that students learn not just from the instructional process itself, which is, of course, the essential core of our business, but also from our attitudes, testimonials, mentoring, and working with students in various roles. Any modern-day appraisal framework must acknowledge and render visible the multiple dimensions of being an educator, and assess teachers not just based on expected learning outcomes, but also on other equally important dimensions of the learning process. In the same way that we want to cater to the needs of each and every learner, a good appraisal system will bring to the surface the talents of each and every teacher. Anyone who has spent many years in schools has known effective teachers who may not be the school's best instructors, but who positively impact students in ways that are more profound and long lasting.

The 21st century also casts doubt on the practice of having absolute standards for success, and students' results on standardized test scores, a measuring rod that most teachers are mercilessly subjected to, are clearly not indicative of the whole picture. A comprehensive modern appraisal system must incorporate various more flexible parameters that define proficient performance, and, eventually, and in sync with the 21st-century trend for education, become almost customized.

In our quest for a better appraisal system, one issue can be addressed—that of authenticity. Teachers rightfully complain that judgment is passed based on specific observations that are only very partial views of the whole picture, and that, for good or for bad, whenever an administrator steps into the classroom for the full length of a lesson, it immediately becomes artificial. Technology comes to the rescue in providing administrators with the means to record more informal, shorter observations based on walk-throughs. Many networked software packages and specific frameworks have been developed that enable administrative teams to walk around the schools, pop into classrooms briefly, or simply record observations after making their rounds. This allows for the independent gathering of a wealth of data about pedagogy, engagement, teaching techniques, use of available resources, and instructional strategies, and at the end of the period, these observations are collated together by the software so that teachers can be provided with extensive evidence of their performance. Many of these software products also feature versions that can be used on smart phones, so that administrators can register their observations on the fly and then sync them with the networked application.

In terms of school improvement and adherence to the new-school model, teachers' readiness to change as required by school guidelines must be an integral part of any evolved appraisal process. As teachers gradually shift from their center-stage role to one that gives the students more responsibility for their own learning, the degree and extent to which teachers lead this effort must be incorporated into any renewed teacher evaluation framework.

THE CORPORATE WAR

Regardless of geographical location, language, and the nature of the system itself, all school systems share a commonality: they are ultimately governed by decision-making bodies that are made up of non-educators who, in most cases, come from the corporate ranks. School administrators and principals are fighting a constant battle to resist the indiscriminate application of corporate dogma to schools.

The role of the leader is always to juggle multiple responsibilities. Protecting the organization against or mitigating the effect of these well-meaning but ill-advised efforts to evangelize educators on the benefits of doing things the corporate way often ranks near the top of the list of causes for job-related headaches.

One would think that, given the recent track record of corporations, many of which barely survived (or failed to survive) a self-created global crisis that took the world economy to the brink of disaster, corporate executives in their school fiduciary incarnations would be a little more tentative in imposing these models on educational organizations. However, despite the growing volume of management literature that calls for a complete overhaul of some of the outdated methods and structures used in the business world, these phased-out models are often still imposed upon education.

In his book *The World is Open* (2009), Curtis Bonk quotes Richard Straub, a director at the European Foundation for Management Development, as saying that "management structures are opening up with values such as empowerment, tolerance, lifelong learning, participation, cooperation, and individual freedom. This is a significant departure from the traditional top-down command-and-control hierarchies that often fueled the exploitation and general distrust of the workers, bureaucratic governments, and overregulation."

And if it was always irritating to deal with the shortsightedness of trying to impose an ill-fitting, rigidly structured model on the infinitely more dynamic and complex environment of schools, the 21st-century scenario makes it even more of a gross mismatch.

In effect, the highly structured, reward-and-punishment-oriented model that was the norm in businesses in the 20th century falls flat in the face of the leadership challenges faced by school administrators in the 21st century. Schools are more organic than organized, and attempts at describing the thriving complex reality of educational institutions via organizational flowcharts, scorecard indicators, and other instruments born in boardroom strategy sessions are a waste of time and energy, the two most scarce and precious resources for leaders.

Larry Cuban, a Stanford University professor and well-known educational author and thinker, relates an often-cited and compelling story in his aptly titled book *The Blackboard and the Bottom Line: Why Schools Can't Be Businesses* (2005). Jamie Vollmer, the manager of a very successful ice-cream company, is admonishing a group of public school educators about the inefficiencies in how the schools are run, and tells them how if he managed his company in that way he would not be in business for too long. After he finishes, he opens up for questions and a woman in the audience asks him whether the ice cream he produces is good, and he answers that it is the best in America. Then she springs the trap, and asks what their policy is when a truck comes into his factory with milk that is not up to their quality standards. Even though he can see what's coming, he truthfully answers that the truck is rejected. She then replies that the difference is that, in education, we take them all, however they come, and do not reject anybody.

Jamie Vollmer had a harsh awakening after that meeting and went on to become an advocate for public schools, and even authored a book entitled *Schools Cannot Do It Alone: Building Public Support for America's Public Schools* (2010), but his story, sadly, is the exception. If anything, trends in management are shifting the focus of businesses more to rediscovering the value of an organization's mission, focusing on people, rekindling intrinsic motivation, and the increasing volume of literature dedicated to spirituality in the workplace, but schools are still subjected to die-hard top-down management theories.

Clearly, there is a pressing need for leadership at the governance level to undergo some deep and long-overdue soul-searching in order to come up with ideas that genuinely assist schools in this difficult transition process rather than hindering them by refusing to acknowledge the fundamental difference that exists between the corporate environment and the education sector.

THE 21ST CENTURY WANTS YOU!

One of the great problems with leadership in schools is finding younger teachers who are willing and have the necessary attributes to emerge out of the ranks and volunteer for a leadership role.

The general misconception about leadership roles being positions of power naturally draws out the more ambitious types, thus reinforcing the stereotype that worked well in the old context: school administrators who loomed large over the organization, and accumulated responsibility and power in equal proportions. Many leadership failures stem out of this flawed motivation for becoming leaders. School leaders who are out there for the perks and the power are likely to embark on a self-defeating journey.

The 21st-century need for authenticity thankfully brings to the surface the need for a new kind of leadership. Andy Hargreaves (2010), author and professor of education at Boston College, summarizes the problem with great clarity: "We need to bear in mind that this trust [that leaders received from staff members] was often blind. In the 21st century, we cannot presume trust; it has to be earned."

Traditionally, school administrators grew out of the cadre of the best practitioners—those teachers who produce the best results, not just in standardized test scores, but in terms of how students relate to them, and the mark they have left on the community during their years on the job. This quasi-Darwinian natural selection method served well enough until the current time, since the teachers who eventually became administrators had to elevate themselves by making themselves visible in some way or other, an attribute that was considered desirable in a leader.

However—and going back again to the example of Level 5 leaders, who are not fueled by ambition for themselves, but rather for the cause—detecting and promoting these leaders is no longer an obvious endeavor. There are many examples in history of great leaders who took the helm despite their lack of interest in doing so, and there is an apparent contradiction in that some of the desirable traits of the 21st-century leader, such as a focus on the things that really matter, genuine love of learning, and selflessness, may hinder ideal candidates by making them think they are not capable of assuming the role. Spotting these promising leaders must be a deliberate strategy, and generating situations in which potential future leaders may showcase their talents is a must for schools. Retreats, team-building activities, group reflections, study groups, and other not-so-conventional professional development strategies can prove to be great breeding grounds for right-brained leaders.

LEADING FOR THE FUTURE

It would be unrealistic to ignore the fact that the ability to successfully lead, especially in the educational context, can only be born out of a deep desire to be of service. The ultimate definition of leadership, for both the 20th and 21st centuries, is that leadership is service, and leaders with a service mindset are sure to adapt to all environments.

The 21st century calls for leaders who have vision, who thrive when sharing responsibility and power, who are not afraid of complexity, who can embrace change, and who enjoy being in schools and being very much a part of the learning process. In the same way that we call for teachers to relinquish the central role and make the students protagonists of their own learning, leaders of the future will have to do the same, shying away from the spotlight to focus on capacity-building for their teams, and modeling a complex and sometimes overwhelming environment that allows for individual expression.

But, ultimately, what sets these leaders apart is their ability to imagine the future, and to inspire the people they lead. Former German chancellor Konrad Adenauer said, "We all live under the same sky, but we don't all have the same horizon." The 21st century presents us with a limitless, infinite horizon, and it is up to those who truly want to lead to head towards it, knowing that even though the horizon will never be attainable, it will still be well worth the journey.

CHAPTER SEVEN

The Building
of the Future

I T IS CLEAR THAT THE MAIN DRIVERS FOR CHANGE are associated with profound transformations in the teacher mindset, a focus on life-long learning, and the development of a completely new pedagogy that takes advantage of infinite opportunities for learning. However, anybody who walks into a classroom can tell that there are things about the physical space used for teaching that also need to change.

Richard Elmore (2006), a Harvard University professor and well-known author, emphasizes the importance of setting up spaces in ways that clearly embody the core business at hand. He gives the example of how fast-food chains and many other businesses are designed in such a way that from the moment a customer steps in, they know what is going on.

CELLS AND BELLS

Most current classrooms are not designed for a 21st-century pedagogy. Despite the many advances and new techniques, like in the Rip van Winkle story, anybody who had taken a 100-year nap would immediately recognize classrooms: rows of desks facing a teacher and a board for the teacher to write on. And even though the main onus for change is on us educators, the learning spaces and schools' general configuration can either become powerful catalysts for or barriers to the development of a new pedagogy. In the same way that if we keep on centering our assessments on sit-down written tests we cannot expect students to be interested in anything other than "what goes on the test," we cannot really expect teachers to implement profound changes if the physical layout of their classrooms is conducive to the old model of teaching rather than the new one.

Schools still operate under the "cells and bells" model: students sit in rectangular rooms for all of their lessons, which are punctuated by bells. The rooms are designed for teacher-centered learning, and there is little or no flexibility for configuring them otherwise.

LEARNING SPACES FOR 21ST-CENTURY EDUCATION

In order to better understand how to create or reconfigure learning spaces for the new paradigm, it is necessary to revisit the drivers for change, so as to identify how to best adapt learning spaces to new modalities of learning.

In his book *Education Nation* (2010), Milton Chen cites British design guru Sean McDougall, who says of the inadequacies of today's learning spaces, "Victorian schools were designed to meet the particular needs of the Victorian era. They were created to turn out 'obedient specialists': adults who could work in factories, assembling components or as domestic servants, not people who needed to think for themselves."

So the pertinent question is, how can we physically transform schools so that the classrooms better enable the learners to develop the traits and capacities that we have identified as essential for the 21st century?

SCHOOL AS AN ORGANIC MODEL

It is time for school administrators to start thinking about how different designs can help catalyze the new model of education. Conceiving the school building as a less predictable, more flexible environment can be the first step towards breaking away from a rigid model and mindset for schools.

As with most aspects of 21st-century education, there are no right or wrong answers, but rather a set of design ideas, guidelines, and criteria that attempt to match the prevailing trends of 21st-century education with designs that schools can adopt in their current or future refurbishing efforts.

SMALL LEARNING COMMUNITIES

Since learning should be customized as much as possible to allow all students to rise up to their full potential, mass-production-type schools are clearly counterproductive, so when population dynamics or budget needs dictate the need for schools with large numbers of students, the tendency is to break them down into what are now known as Small Learning Communities (SLCs).

This is a newer term for what school planners have long been doing in their attempts to break down larger numbers of students into manageable groups, and the concept of SLCs is now also reflected in building design. Administrators are challenged to think about what the ideal unit of learning would be, as well as what the ideal size for each SLC that can be supervised, mentored, and guided by adults in the building would be. Some trends go towards cross-age SLCs, while other schools retain the traditional age-level communities as the fundamental unit for instruction.

Whatever the decision and the name given to it, the concept of dividing large student numbers into smaller, more manageable learning units is essential, and school spaces must be able to reflect the identity of each community, in order to clearly provide its members with a sense of belonging.

The Four-Spaces Metaphor

Perhaps one of the best metaphors for 21st-century learning environments is that of the four primordial spaces that David Thornburg, a designer, author, and futurist, referred to in a paper published in 1997. In his essay, which is forward thinking enough to still be relevant even though it was written in the previous century, David Thornburg defines four essential dimensions of learning spaces.

The **campfire** is where the campers (the students) learn from stories that are being told, and, as such, preserves the lecturing, or teacher-centered, dimension of learning, which must still be present in the new school, albeit not overwhelmingly dominant, as it was in the old school. The campfire image also serves to emphasize the ancestral nature of the art of storytelling, which is an important part of life in a learning community, and the idea of the light of the central fire illuminating learning. The campfire, by definition, is a public, community space, thus reinforcing the idea that lecturing, or the transfer of information from the teacher or an invited guest, should not happen between the four walls of a classroom. Some of the modern design attempts in schools incorporate the campfire space, in the form of amphitheater-like seating or a small auditorium, at the physical center of the small learning community, so that it becomes a shared activity. Given the advances in telecommunications that have torn down the walls of schools, campfire learning can also be present in the form of distance learning via teleconference, with the added value of beaming worldwide experts into the learning community.

The **watering hole** also constitutes a very powerful image for peer learning. Again, rooted deep in the tradition of travelers' journeys and even animal herd behavior, the watering hole is a compelling representation of how students also learn when they congregate at places that favor the casual, more relaxed environment associated with eating and drinking. The huge success of more comfortable coffee shop environments is a lesson as to the power and attractiveness of such spaces, as are the bookstore cafés. The inclusion of café-like small spaces in schools, or even certain corners where students can congregate and work together, not only provides a venue for community learning in a more relaxed environment, but also facilitates collaboration.

Cave space also appeals to a very primeval desire for reflection, and, in this case, helps to embody quiet areas for independent individual studies. Hitherto reserved for designated areas within the school library, modern school designs include quiet cave-like study areas that provide independent but visually supervised spaces that allow students to engage in independent study during or after the school day.

Finally, what Thornburg calls **life** reflects all learning environments that allow for hands-on learning through real-life experience. Laboratories, outdoor experimentation areas, simulation labs, workshops, and a long list of similar spaces have always been present in schools, encouraging students to learn through doing, which, as any educator will attest, is not only the learning modality that students enjoy the most, but also the one that yields the most significant gains in learning.

No More Classrooms

We are not forecasting the demise of the classroom per se, but the word *classroom* is almost inexorably linked to mental images of symmetrical rooms with desks and benches facing a teacher lecturing. With the goal of focusing more on learning than teaching, schools are progressively moving towards the concept of the learning studio. Learning studios are irregularly shaped (either directly through construction, or indirectly through interior design), and provide for smaller breakout spaces that are geared towards smaller group activities rather than teacher lecturing.

Regardless of the actual name for the space, a good starting point for 21st-century design is to provide learning environments that are not pointing to the teacher, and that allow flexibility and multiple configurations within the same lesson.

INSIDE OR OUTSIDE
THE LEARNING STUDIOS

Another interesting evolution in learning environments concerns how much of the learning process occurs inside the "classroom" and how much occurs in shared "public" areas. One of the sacrosanct principles of the old school is that when the teacher closes the door of the classroom, what happens in it remains largely shielded from the public eye and is the exclusive prerogative of the teacher. The advent of professional learning communities and a call for teachers to effectively collaborate and share good practice has increased awareness of the need to open up the classrooms.

This manifests itself in the transparency of the learning environment, not only in terms of monitoring and supervision from the outside in, but also with a view towards allowing the teacher in charge to send students out into the common centralized spaces for breakout activities or use of specialized facilities. These commons, or central spaces, may contain some of the informal "watering hole" areas that double up as outflow spaces for differentiated learning, as well as the use of more expensive equipment that can then be shared by the whole Small Learning Community. Modern school designs tend to incorporate large central agora-type spaces within the core of each SLC in order to accommodate this form of learning.

It is also interesting to think about how outdoor areas can be integrated with the inside learning environment. Especially in areas with a more benign climate, the use of gardens, porch-type small work areas and other outdoor spaces is an important design consideration. Some schools are exemplars in their use of these spaces as natural extensions of the learning environment. Brookside Elementary, within the Cranbrook School of Art campus in the greater Detroit area, and Crow Island School near Chicago are masterful examples of how gardens and green areas can be more than a buffer for learning, and constitute full-fledged learning spaces in their own right.

RECONFIGURABLE SPACES

Another factor in the design of school spaces for the 21st century is the fact that we will be planning for a future that is uncertain. Predicting trends in education is difficult, and fast-paced changes demand that learning environments not be hardwired in ways that result in limiting them to a single use. Movable walls and sliding panels, retractable bleachers, and many other changeable features enable the reconfiguration of learning spaces. With the exception of perhaps science, a subject area that requires a degree of specificity that perforce might need to result in fixed design decisions, most learning environments should allow for multiples uses, not only from one academic year to another, but also, on occasion, within the same term.

ENVIRONMENTAL STEWARDSHIP

At this point in time, schools need to do much more than just pay lip service to an environmental conscience—they must act on it. There are many activities related to recycling, saving energy, and other "green" initiatives that can be undertaken in a building, but if schools want to really get serious, they need to back up their environmental actions with design features that embody the concept of sustainability.

The LEED standard (Leadership in Energy and Environmental Design, www.usgbc.org/LEED) is a set of norms that buildings can comply with in order to attain a green certification, and that involve different levels (bronze, gold, and platinum) depending on the level of compliance with water recycling measures, constructing with recycled materials, and a series of other environmental features that even involve waste recycling through wetlands. A school's compliance with LEED standards can serve as a great catalyst for increasing the level of environmental awareness of the community.

Whether or not a school chooses to comply with LEED, it is essential that students are confronted on an ongoing basis with systems in the building that incorporate the concept of environmental stewardship. If electricity-generating solar panels are still prohibitively expensive, some simpler rain collection tanks, green roofs or gardens, or other less costly schemes can prove to be powerful symbols that steer students towards a greener conscience.

Also, because sustainability is a strategy that is difficult to argue against, it can be a good bridge to the community.

UBIQUITOUS TECHNOLOGY

Schools have invested vast amounts of money in technology, including big computer labs full of wired desktop stations connected to the Internet. These labs are a common fixture in most schools, and smaller siblings of them can also be found in libraries within school buildings.

However, in the 21st century, portability and wireless capabilities are the norm, and there seems to be no longer a need for traditional computer labs with their neat rows of computers facing the teachers.

As laptops become more powerful and less expensive, and smart phones become increasingly indistinguishable from personal computers, technology in schools will go mobile, and follow students and teachers in their learning. Some applications, such as video editing, will still require the faster processing speed of desktop computers as well as large flat screens, but by and large, technology, like learning itself, will become more ubiquitous and decentralized.

BUILDING AS A 3D TEXTBOOK

Another relatively innovative characteristic of modern school buildings is the purposeful highlighting of maintenance and other systems so as to explicitly utilize them as learning opportunities for the students. Some of the structural systems are intentionally left open to view, and environmental control features can be tweaked and maintained by the students themselves as learning opportunities.

The building, therefore, is used as a three-dimensional textbook in which students learn hands-on about the subsystems of the structure, and it would not be out of the question, for example, to give senior students (under supervision) some degree of monitoring and control over the environmental system at the school.

CREATIVITY AND IMAGINATION

Creativity and imagination are not only paramount skills in the 21st century, but also two of the skills that are more at risk given the overabundance of ready-made solutions and the fact that so much is available and taken for granted that there seems to be little need to really create anything.

But schools are not buildings that abound in spaces that foster creativity and imagination. And the well-known architectural principle that form follows function, although certainly not always respected in school buildings, in this case points to the need to provide specific spaces that are tailored towards developing creativity and imagination.

Certainly much can be achieved through interior design and equipment, but there are also structural changes that can create specific spaces for creativity and imagination. Black-box theaters are slowly making their way into schools. These "black boxes" are literally black rooms that combine a stage, lights, and the rest of the equipment needed for a theater, with a more or less empty space ample enough for improvisation, rehearsals, and other activities that seek to develop creativity in an austere, "blank canvas" context that allows students to focus on their creative forces without any unnecessary distractions. Although conceived primarily for use within the performing arts, the demand for black boxes will increase for other disciplines, and also for use by staff in their professional development, since the golden rule applies that we cannot ask our students to develop what we are not. Contrary to the self-effacing preconception that most people embrace—that creativity is a naturally endowed gift—it can be taught, fostered, and developed like any other skill for both the students and the adults in the building, who can awaken their own creativity through directed professional development.

The existence of such spaces is also important in the context of the ease with which consumers can now jump into the role of producers, or "prosumers," given the availability of state-of-the-art software that allows the common user to generate movies or other creative multimedia projects.

A building that caters to the creative side of students and staff members can certainly make things more lively, attractive, and fun. A well-known experiment in Sweden attempted to prove the "fun theory" (www.thefuntheory.com, from auto maker Volkswagen) by converting stairs into an interactive musical keyboard, in order to entice passersby in a metro station to use the stairs instead of the escalator (a healthier, and more environmentally friendly, choice). The fact that each step produced the sound of a musical note resulted in the stairs being used 66 percent more than they were without the interactive piano.

IMMERSIVE LEARNINGSCAPE

The design of the Immersive Learningscape strives to address three key challenges to current classroom design:

1. how to provide high levels of flexibility in educational spaces for today's and future needs,

2. learning and teaching of 21st-century skills, and

3. how to facilitate multiple modalities of learning.

This case study is designed as a "landscape of learning and immersive moments" targeting active learning, teamwork, collaboration, interdisciplinary learning, and communication skills. The design introduces spaces that allow specificity of activity and flexibility of group sizes, from the individual research spaces, to large classes for imparting education.

The design (see Figure 1) takes a typical and ubiquitous double-loaded corridor classroom wing and turns it into a dynamic and forward-thinking education environment. Within it, systems (mechanical, electrical, data) are carried under a raised floor allowing for future modification of the space as needs arise. The interior spaces are broken into five typologies of learning (Think, Create, Discover, Impart, and Exchange), which cater to the different 21st-century skills needed to be acquired to compete in a global marketplace. This design allows for multiple modalities of learning, from large group zones, to hands-on spaces, to technology-facilitated, small- and large-team project-based learning rooms, to individual private "cocoons" for deep thinking and researching.

Bringing all the teachers to the core in an open environment enables the curriculum to shift from one delivered in silos, to a more integrated and holistic curriculum delivery.

LEARNING THROUGH INTERACTIONS

One of the main postulates of the Reggio Emilia approach to schooling is that of learning through interactions. And much of the success and rel-

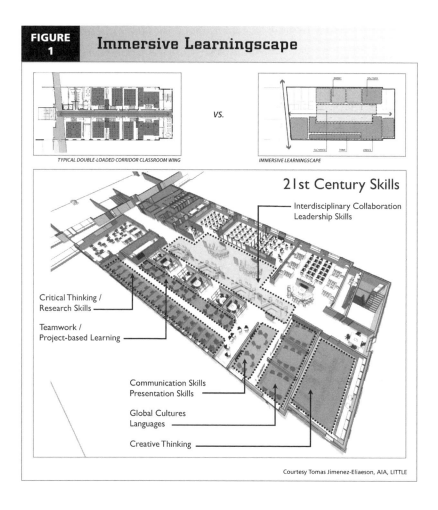

FIGURE 1

Immersive Learningscape

VS.

TYPICAL DOUBLE-LOADED CORRIDOR CLASSROOM WING

IMMERSIVE LEARNINGSCAPE

21st Century Skills

Interdisciplinary Collaboration
Leadership Skills

Critical Thinking /
Research Skills

Teamwork /
Project-based Learning

Communication Skills
Presentation Skills

Global Cultures
Languages

Creative Thinking

Courtesy Tomas Jimenez-Eliaeson, AIA, LITTLE

evancy of this movement in recent years has to do with the fact that the 21st-century scenario, less intent on accumulating factual knowledge, lends itself increasingly to experiential, hands-on, interactive learning.

Museums are a good example of a shift to 21st-century thinking—modern-day exhibits have evolved from their former passive and protected role into a more interactive role: visitors can learn by experimenting, touching, and playing around. This model, which has proved so effective and appealing that very few of these venerable institutions do not include hands-on exhibits, can also be extended to schools. There are no doubts as to the benefits of having dynamic, inter-active exhibits for each content area within the physical layout of the school that allow children of all ages (including the adults) to learn through interaction. A great example of this modality of learning is the Henry Ford Academy in Dearborn, Michigan, adjoining the museum of the same name, that features 12 acres of exhibits that include, amongst other things, the bus in which Rosa Parks made her famous protest and the chair in which Abraham Lincoln was sitting when he was assassi-nated. Students at the school are actively involved with these exhibits several times a week, as part of their regular learning activities (www.edutopia.org).

PROJECT-BASED LEARNING

Because we are accustomed to the regular structure of departmental or age-level classrooms, and teachers residing in and taking possession of rooms, the notion of designing with collaboration in mind seems counterintuitive.

One of the most difficult issues that school designers have to con-tend with is the tension between the desire to provide each subject area with its own proprietary space that can be designed and customized to teach that content area to the best extent possible, and the unstoppable trend towards interdisciplinary learning, moving away from the artifi-cial compartmentalization of subject areas that schools have instituted in students' and teachers' minds as a byproduct of curriculum design and standards.

Some technical high schools have been able to break away from the traditional center of gravity of the content area, and have created learn-ing environments specifically designed for project-based learning. These spaces are centered around the project at hand, which is clearly visible and dominates the physical space, so that they can be reconfig-ured periodically based on the new projects to be tackled. Achieving a suitable tradeoff between the specific needs of disciplinary areas and the need for a more integrated, interdisciplinary education model is an elusive equilibrium, but definitely must be addressed in efforts to re-create or adapt schools for the new paradigm.

COMFORTABLE FURNITURE

Another archetypical fixture of schools is that students not only must endure the torture of having to sit passively listening to the teacher lecture for far too many hours a day, but also must do so in very uncomfortable chairs. This is based on one of the unspoken principles of school: students should not be very comfortable in class, lest they get too cozy and fall asleep.

At this point in the evolution of education, we should discard these repressive ideas, and should think of how furniture can assist, rather than restrict, the learning process. School furniture, and especially chairs, should not only be comfortable and follow ergonomic designs as much as possible, but also allow students to move and stretch. It is inhumane, and certainly unhealthy for their bodies, to force students to sit still on rigid chairs for hours on end. Modern chairs feature more ergonomic shapes and flexible materials that allow students to move and vary their postures without needing to get up.

LIBRARIES, MEDIA CENTERS, OR NOTHING?

Another ongoing discussion amongst facility planners has to do with whether it is really necessary to include a traditional library in modern school buildings. Most schools no longer call them libraries, but rather media centers, and in their various modern incarnations, these spaces are the heart and soul of many school buildings, and principals are diligent in mentioning their efforts to rally staff and students to make good and extensive use of them.

In their current generalized versions, media centers combine book racks, rows of desktop computers for research, and breakout rooms for smaller-group research or seminar activities led by staff members. On many occasions, the library also hosts distance learning rooms fully set up for videoconferencing.

However, at the risk of committing educational blasphemy, I submit that the need for these centers of learning should be questioned. If we agree that one of the fundamental tenets of 21st-century education is that learning occurs anywhere and everywhere, and that technology follows learning ubiquitously, it is valid to ask if there is a real necessity for an area within the school where learning occurs by design. And that question is not as innocuous as it may seem at first glance: there might be a powerful implicit message sent by earmarking a particular area in the building for learning—a message that may undermine the overarching goal of having a school building where learning occurs throughout the physical environment.

As with many of the other issues to be faced when addressing the challenge of 21st-century education, there is no right or wrong answer. Each community will find and develop what best suits its own particular reality. But, at least, the question is one that should be carefully analyzed.

COMMUNITY CONNECTION

Because of the fact that in this century students will be global players in an interconnected world, making sure that they learn to live in community and affirm their strong local identity is fundamentally important.

The best schools of the future will truly be open to the local community, as a way to regain a prominent societal role as well as to allow students to interact with the local community and receive value from it.

In *The Third Teacher* (OWP/P Architecture, 2010), a wonderful compilation of resources about how design can enhance the learning process, the authors bring attention to the issue of the relationship of schools with the community: "Both the fortress and bubble schools are based on the premise that communities, particularly those in challenging urban contexts, have low social capital" (Riley, 2008).

There have been strong and explicit reactions against both "bubble" and "fortress" schools, both of which are based on isolating the school community from the outside environment, whether on issues that have to do with safety (hence the fortress) or by artificially creating an internal system, the bubble, that is markedly different from the prevailing social environment. Detractors say they have a negative impact on children during their formative years. Sharing sports facilities, halls, performing arts spaces, and any other area of the school that can be opened up to the community is of great importance, especially if students can also participate in that connection, either through showcasing their work or though service to the community itself.

Spaces for Education

But ultimately, all in all, school spaces will be what people make of them. Schools are places that come alive in ways that are unforeseen by planners and occupants alike, and that serve to build upon that profound visceral connection that people have with each other in education.

The use, design, and configuration of spaces within schools constitute very personal and unique decisions for every educational community. But what emerges very clearly is that a 21st-century pedagogy can only be developed and implemented within spaces that need to be reconfigured from the industrial model of desks facing the teacher. And, in an inversion of a primary principle of architecture, at least in education, function also follows form.

CHAPTER EIGHT

School Systems
of the Future

A RECURRING THEME THROUGHOUT THIS BOOK is that there are a number of disconnects between what we know is best in educational terms, and current practice in schools. And one of the most evident discrepancies between what educators think is right and what happens in schools has to do with standardized testing, and with the issue of how to enforce systems of accountability through centralized supervision.

There practically isn't any instance in which education is being discussed, formally or informally, in which teachers and administrators do not express their dissatisfaction with the constraints they face on behalf of standards and, especially, mounting pressure to raise scores on standardized tests that, at best, only measure some dimensions of student learning. When transposed with an international setting, teachers similarly focus their woes on international systems of examinations and their omnipresent influence on the curriculum. I attended a presentation at the NECC (National Educational Computing Conference) in 2006 in San Diego, during which a presenter was talking about accountability systems. He gave every attendee a pair of disposable 3D glasses like the ones you get in the movies, and, after showing on the screen a spreadsheet filled with scores from standardized tests, he asked us to put on the 3D glasses, as he was going to show us in 3D the teaching strategies that led to such high scores and the success of the school in question. When we all had donned our glasses, a 3D text emerged from behind the scores, reading "TEACH TO THE TEST!"

Even taking into account the fact that we educators are not always the most positive and optimistic bunch of professionals in the workplace, and that nobody really likes to be measured externally, there is still some basis for the perpetual dissatisfaction of teachers with external measures of accountability and their effect on teaching and learning practices. When these systems meet the 21st-century education model, with its underlying focus on customization and intrinsic drive to break away from a one-size-fits-all model of education, there is quite a clash.

THE ACCOUNTABILITY CHAIN

The whole focus of state standards, standardized tests, and international examinations is on accountability, and making sure that students learn what is required as they go through the school system. This need to standardize is not exclusive to education; most professions include some form of centralized control over procedures and standards, but most likely not to the extent to which the teaching profession is subjected to uniform expectations.

School districts not only pool centralized resources and provide support for schools, but also focus much of their work on making sure that the instructional process conforms to general and sometimes very specific directives and guidelines for schools and teachers. Standards, at whatever level they apply depending on the educational system at stake, prescribe subjects and skills that teachers need to address during the school curriculum for each age level and content area.

Completing this accountability chain, standardized tests, with their associated rewards and incentives, ensure that students have learned according to standards and that they have done so in a certain period of time, the academic year.

In the international arena, international examination systems, such as the very traditional Cambridge exams (the original "O" and "A" levels have now morphed into IGCSE and AICE) or the more progressive International Baccalaureate, supplement school programs and provide international benchmarks that school administrators use to validate their respective programs and to rate the academic excellence of their schools.

It is probably not productive to attempt to discern the reasons for the public's need to hold teachers accountable for their instruction to such painstaking levels, since that discussion would, in all likelihood, only bring up the prejudicial views members of the public have about teachers and schools. But a question looms in the minds of all educators who are faced with decisions about what to teach when the standards are, in their judgment, not the most pertinent for their students: "Is there a real need for a universal, uniform set of contents and expectations for all students in all schools, or could teachers, administrators, and schools make their own decisions as to what works best for their students?"

What's Wrong with It All?

There is a profound and unanimous rejection by teachers of any system of accountability on which they are measured. State, national, and international standards, school accountability systems, teacher appraisals—they are all universally vilified by teachers. Teachers are intent on assessing students, but when they themselves are controlled or assessed, it triggers an indiscriminate loathing of all accountability systems.

It is worthwhile to analyze why standards, standardized testing, and other centralized monitoring and supervision systems generate so many negative reactions in educators, with the view of trying to discern how the general accountability framework for schools may evolve to be compatible with the new paradigm.

Standardization: Educators rightfully complain that, even though the benefits of universal standards and benchmarking are obvious in that they ensure that all students are taught a certain minimum amount of information and skills, and that they reach certain performance levels, it is known that not all students evolve alike and that their needs and learning styles will necessarily differ. Thus, the one-size-fits-all model of education reinforced by rigorous standards will never be agreeable to teachers, and all efforts in that direction will always be met with skepticism. At the end of the day, despite planners' best efforts to incorporate modern pedagogy or any other educational advances, standards are standard, and they will apply indiscriminately to each and every child, which we know to be counter to current knowledge about educational best practice.

Nature of standardized testing: The idea of all students taking the same fixed-duration, sit-down written test on a certain immovable date, often a test that includes multiple-choice questions graded by computers, is abhorrent to educators. And yet, for the most part, standardized tests are exactly that oppressive form of assessment. While the whole world of education leans towards formative, customized assessment instruments, the major decider on a child's future, as well as the main instrument by which school effectiveness is gauged, consists of a summative and rigid written evaluation. So far, accountability and benchmarking have taken precedence over sound educational practice, and it seems that the only way to ascertain the quality of instruction is to test all students the same way, and targeting just one dimension of education: academic learning. The No Child Left Behind Act in the United States and other national standards and testing systems in other countries, as well as international examinations, have exacerbated the pressure that educators feel when faced with these external constraints. These systems have caused educators, in ways that are inevitable as well as unspoken, to gear the instructional process primarily to making sure students perform well on the tests. The OECD/CERI report on assessment for learning (2008) specifically addresses this issue: "In environments where summative tests have high visibility, teachers often feel compelled to 'teach to the test,' and students are encouraged to meet performance goals (to perform well on tests) at the expense of learning goals (to understand and master new knowledge)."

Centralized leadership not in touch with school reality: Another reasonable objection to centralized structures is the fact that, especially in larger districts or school systems, it is impossible for district leaders to really be in touch with all that occurs at schools and devise solutions that work best for each particular educational community. Perhaps an equilibrium needs to be achieved between external requirements and their impact on teaching and learning, and how each classroom teacher can adapt/tweak/modify these requirements to make them relevant in the classroom setting. But that equilibrium is elusive by definition if teachers are to be judged exclusively based on test scores, and when schools are threatened with closure if they do not show required improvements on those results. The human instinct for survival will shift the teaching and learning process primarily towards test require- ments under those conditions. If a standardized test is to drive instruc- tion, it will inexorably lead to blanket solutions that are not tailored to the individual needs and learning styles of students.

Individual nature of assignments, no collaboration: Overwhelm- ingly, standards, expectations, and tests are geared towards the individ- ual. Some notable exceptions in international examinations include a coursework component that is carried out in groups, but that only impacts a small fraction of the grades. The real world functions on proj- ects that are collaborative, and the value of developing the skill to effec- tively work together is unquestionable. Under the basic premise of identifying the individual contributions of students for the sake of accountability, learners are evaluated independently, and standards are developed exclusively with individuals in mind. It is uncommon as of yet to see standards that focus on group skills, attributes, or perfor- mance, or that expect each student to become an effective collaborator.

Stigmatization of mistakes: We all know that making mistakes is a part of the learning process, and eminent speakers and thinkers have long said that there is a need to redesign our educational system so that it encourages creative approaches and does not stigmatize mistakes. In his first book, *Out of Our Minds: Learning to be Creative* (2001), Ken Robinson specifically addresses the shortcomings of conventional assessment: "Insensitive assessment can damage students' creativity and may encourage them to take a safe option, avoiding experimentation and never finding how to learn and correct their mistakes." In effect, assessments are often designed to penalize mistakes. Most teachers remember multiple-choice tests on which points were deducted for wrong answers and students ended up with negative scores. It is inevitable, then, that teachers and learners will tend to play it safe and be as conservative as possible in all approaches to preparing for stan- dardized tests.

BEYOND STANDARDS
AND ACCOUNTABILITY

It seems that when schools are envisioning the future—the new 21st-century educational model and its challenge to reinvent teaching and learning—that would also be a good opportunity to take a second look at standards and at the concept of accountability in general.

In the face of such fundamental changes, conventional wisdom must be challenged. The whole principle of accountability in schools should be reassessed in the context of analyzing education for the future. I was told recently about a group of American educators who went on a study tour to better understand the school system in Finland. Finland, possibly together with Singapore, is hailed as one of the leading nations in terms of their educational system, because they select the best and brightest for the teaching profession (and reward them accordingly). Upon meeting with some of their Finnish counterparts, the American educators were asked why they had this obsession with accountability. In Finland, the local educators explained, they prefer to focus on responsibility, and on ensuring that teachers have the internal drive and motivation to get the job done properly—consequently, they do not need such extensive accountability systems.

Not every effective educational practice can be copied directly or transposed onto a completely different setting. But it is true that while external systems of measurement and control can be effective for as long as they are in place and enforced in a system of rewards and punishments, a true mindset change comes from the inside out, and not the other way round.

Daniel Pink, in his book *Drive* (2009), cites research that shows that in the complex, nonlinear, open-ended 21st-century scenario, people who try to find answers lured by the promise of rewards do not perform as well as those who are compelled to do so by their own drive (hence the title of the book) and internal motivation.

Psychologist Barry Schwartz, author of *The Paradox of Choice*, delivered a fascinating talk on "The Loss of Wisdom" at the TED conference (February 2009). During his address, he also took a stab at the educational system, referring to standards by saying, "Scripted education prevents disasters, but what it also does is ensure mediocrity." Furthermore, he added, "Excessive dependence on incentives demoralizes professional activities."

THE CONCEPT OF STANDARDS IN THE 21ST CENTURY

How can we redefine the whole concept of standards and accountability in the knowledge era? The first goal is to change the focus from universal standards that apply equally to all learners to basic fundamental principles that appeal to all educators. Mission and vision, basic sets of values, and the fundamental tenets of 21st-century education, with a focus on lifelong learning, should be the real standards.

Educators must be accountable, perhaps not for teaching specific content and skills, but rather for infusing in their students a love of learning, developing a mindset for lifelong learning, and embodying the values and the mission and vision of the organization.

This seems highly idealistic and countercultural to today's world of measurable outcomes and SMART objectives, but Antoine de Saint-Exupéry, an early 20th-century aviator, adventurer, and author of the children's book *The Little Prince* (1943), comes to our rescue with words of great wisdom: "If you want to build a ship, don't drum up the men to gather wood, divide the work and give orders. Instead, teach them to yearn for the vast and endless sea."

In order to foster internally originated responsibility as opposed to externally mandated outcomes, it makes sense to work on fundamental principles and make sure that teachers embody the vision and objectives of each school and system. However, those qualities are hard to measure and account for, though, in the words of Albert Einstein, "Not everything that can be counted counts, and not everything that counts can be counted."

STANDARDS ANYWAY

But if, despite the fact that they are somewhat counter to the whole notion of 21st-century education, we set out to define standards and evaluate how schools manage to build them into the classroom process, we must, as a first step, define the nature of the beast.

In the old school, standards and the ensuing accountability chain focused on content and skills that were defined with specific outcomes in mind. That model presented clear and almost incontrovertible methods for success; in some cases, even the number of hours allotted to each content area in the curriculum was set in stone. But in the 21st century it is not as easy to determine what the sure road to success is.

So the initial consideration has to do with the object of standards in the new context. Given the dynamic and transient nature of information in the new paradigm, which is characterized by an uncertain future, jobs that have not yet been invented, and evolving disciplines, developing standards that relate to specific content areas will necessitate first that educators in the system define what the core content for each subject area is that students need to master, know, and remember.

This is a question that is seldom asked, but one that education must address continuously. We do not want our students to walk around like broken computer terminals, not really knowing anything once their Internet connections are switched off. But there must be an in-depth study at each school and district about what is really necessary for students to learn, master, and remember in order to be well-informed citizens and cultured individuals, and to have the ability to master higher-order skills. We can say for sure, for example, that it is pointless to remember the exact date of a battle, other than in terms of understanding its relevance within the particular period in time being studied, since that information can easily be found on the Internet, but it is probably important to learn about the context and significance of that battle if it is significant to the cultural identity of that particular community. One would not want a citizen of that community to have to access online sources of information on demand in order to read about the importance of that historical event, since it pertains to that person's sense of identity.

There is a lot of weeding to do in terms of core content in most school systems, and educators' complaints against requiring excessive factual recall are justifiably rooted in disproportionate content and memorization testing. Nonetheless, the decision of what constitutes core content for each system must be made, and will still give rise to a body of core standards.

SKILLS FOR THE 21ST-CENTURY LEARNER

Even though the new paradigm calls for less-specific standards and more focus on lifelong learning, whenever the 21st-century learner is described, the overwhelming focus is on the skills and capabilities to be acquired. There are numerous taxonomies of 21st-century skills that focus on issues such as critical thinking, technological literacy, media literacy, and a long list of other skills to be acquired by this digital generation.

A closed and fixed taxonomy of skills is counter to the 21st-century education model, since the skills to be acquired will change with the times. Defining standards about competencies to be acquired will prove an elusive goal, since the measurement of the acquisition of these skills is necessarily fuzzy.

How can we define and eventually measure whether learners have gone through all the necessary developmental and learning stages in school so that they are ready to emerge as productive citizens of the 21st century?

It seems logical that standards will tend to be defined in terms of tasks to be accomplished by students throughout their learning. These tasks should be defined in ways that cater to different learning styles and abilities, that involve some of the core principles (lifelong learning, collaboration), and that take into account the developmental stages of children. One could imagine a customized portfolio of tasks to be accomplished, which, especially in the older ages, also takes into account the preferences and inclinations of the students themselves.

The accomplishment of these tasks would be marked down and assessed, without the need for a preestablished sequential completion and subsequent levels of proficiency to be attained. Each student's record and performance in accomplishing these tasks would become that student's own personal road map to learning, one that would hopefully be used positively in terms of job placement and higher courses of studies.

There could be some ethical issues about the accessibility of these records, in that a bad performance during one of the attempts to perform these tasks could be used against the student in question many years later, or a certain trait or lack thereof may be similarly used in the future.

In that respect, logs of video games yield some interesting clues as to what standardized testing may look like in the future. Some systems keep a record of how long the game was played, what objectives were accomplished, and in what time, purposefully not registering the number or extent of the errors or failures. One of the major shortcomings of our educational system is the condemnation of mistakes that has inhibited student contributions and resulted in many students not trying, lest they be ridiculed or punished for making mistakes. A new approach to evaluating students' needs is required to guarantee that the learners will feel free to attempt to solve problems as many times as necessary and that they will not be deterred by fear of the consequences of failure.

One possible solution, then, is for standardized testing to evolve from its current maligned incarnation of high-stakes, sit-down written tests into a task-based, multidimensional portfolio targeting various areas of learning that constitutes an individualized road map to graduation. It would be a system that would be less centralized, more flexible, and, as such, probably increasingly challenging in terms of organization for schools and districts. The concept of accountability would be a little more hazy, but the ultimate goal is not that the system becomes absolutely foolproof so that no students wanting to play the system may escape with an undeserved degree, but rather that the learning and prevailing pedagogy become engaging, authentic, and meaningful, so that no students would *want* to take any shortcut, because they have a genuine motivation to learn and do not want to be shortchanged on their education.

INTERNATIONAL EXAMINATIONS

In terms of standardization and accountability, international examination systems provide schools with opportunities to externally reference and validate their programs, as well as compare themselves against internationally recognized standards.

Even though in most cases these organizations see themselves as generating curriculum, and there is extensive ad-hoc documentation to support that claim, the main components of these programs, and by far the most popular, are none other than the good old standardized exams, albeit with an international flavor. Students sit for these exams on the same day all over the world (the Internet and potential associated risks of cross-time-zone plagiarism has forced the writing of different versions of papers), they are centrally marked by specially employed examiners, and numeric results, without any further comments, are returned to students months later, in many countries in time to become a decisive factor for university entrance.

Despite honest efforts from most of these organizations to include coursework and other nonexam components in their programs, if there was an award for the most regressive assessment system, based on the fact that it is absolutely summative, standardized, impersonal, without any possibilities of retesting, and that no feedback is ever given, probably these international exams would be strong candidates for such a dubious accolade.

The principle behind these systems of examinations is that an international organization with high academic standards helps to validate the school's program of studies, and taking away the element of international recognition and validation would gnaw at the very essence of these systems. So how could they evolve? Here are a few suggestions that could also be applied to standardized examinations in general:

Play on the international dimension for collaborative projects: One of the key strengths of these programs is that, at least nominally and, in the case of the International Baccalaureate, to a substantial extent, they are international in their conception and their curriculum. A prominent component of these programs should be the development of collaborative international projects that fall under the organization's umbrella, with the organization providing support in the form of rubrics, learning guides, and other pedagogical background. This not only would encourage collaborative work, and move away from the exclusive and excessive focus on individual work, but also would target the development of skills that have to do with globalization, and possibly with technological literacy, since in order to communicate with their peers and carry on the projects, students will have to use technology extensively.

Computer adaptive tasks: Instead of centering the whole process exclusively on the outcome of sit-down written tests, students should have to progressively complete adaptive tasks on computer-based systems. Of course, the nature of these tasks would be radically different from the ones that currently dominate these exams, which are still content and skills based; the new tasks would include customized simulations, games, and so on. One can imagine that the requirement for passing and/or obtaining a certain grade will be based on how many stages of the simulation are completed, and the scores, to be easily surveyed through game logs. The system may also include impromptu problem-solving scenarios over an extended period of time that require students to collaborate, deal with unexpected problems, create solutions from scratch, analyze and criticize media, and so on—scenarios that help them develop 21st-century skills.

Harness the power of centralized resources: In order to reinvent themselves, educational organizations currently offering these international examinations should channel their resources into bridging the gap between the great thinkers and the classroom via dedicated videoconference sessions tailored to the courses at hand. They should develop state-of-the-art interactive learning experiences that may include virtual reality and a community of international students whose interactions will form part of their portfolio for completing program requirements.

These international organizations are in a position to offer many groundbreaking activities and resources that would add value to school programs.

Create learning communities: Successful examples abound of projects that involve interactions between real-life scientists and researchers and students who supply them with local data (e.g., local weather observations, readings, and measurements), or simply ask questions related to field research that is being performed. These Web-based, quest-type projects allow students to engage in real-life meaningful research and provide all sorts of opportunities to learn and exercise 21st-century learning skills. It could very well be a requirement for successful completion of the international certificate to be awarded that students must participate in a certain number of these projects and contribute to them in ways that are detailed and that will be evaluated by their assigned coach/mentor/supervisor.

FROM VILLAINS TO HEROES?

There are many paths that address the need to change education for the 21st century. But these paths are not always clear, and teachers and administrators struggle not only against the confusing stimuli and intrinsic complexity of the challenge, but also against the numerous external constraints that can be powerful inhibitors to really being innovative and embracing change for the benefit of their students. I have enumerated many of the problems attributed to centralized accountability systems, including standards and standardized testing, but, paradoxically, the field is ripe for centralized systems to become catalysts for change.

For good or for bad, it is an accepted fact that the teaching and learning process is driven by centralized decisions, whether at the district or state level, or by requirements from international examination programs. These organizations, which have earned a dubious reputation by virtue of their regressive practices, can now rise up to the challenge and instill and foster sound educational practices that schools will have to adopt, and thus really become agents for positive change. In this respect, leaders' bold vision, as well as help from nongovernmental educational organizations, can push the agenda towards a gradual reform of the educational system that will encourage similar evolution throughout school systems.

CHAPTER NINE

A Vision for the School of the Future

Wayne Gretzky, one of the greatest ice hockey players of all time, said, "A good hockey player plays where the puck is; a great hockey player plays where the puck is going to be."

There is a marked difference between what most of the players in education know to be the right imperative for school reform and what they can actually do. Even the most progressive administrators cannot afford to be too radical—they must be much more conservative in their actions than in their thinking.

A good example of this difficulty is provided in the book I*magination First: Unlocking the Power of Possibility* (2009), in which authors Eric Liu and Scot Noppe-Brandon use the example of the QWERTY keyboard layout as a metaphor for how obviously beneficial change can be hindered by the costs of reeducating a whole generation. The QWERTY layout, which is quite awkward for entering text, was devised at a time when mechanical typewriters used to frequently jam. The letter layout was conceived to deliberately slow down typists, so as to minimize this irksome jamming. But, at this point, changing the QWERTY layout to an optimized design would entail relearning how to type for an entire generation, and the economic and educational costs are unthinkable.

There are many QWERTY layouts in our schools: fixed schedules, compartmentalized information in subject areas, grouping of students by age, and many other characteristics of schools that we take for granted and that are as immovable as the QWERTY keyboard, despite the fact that we know better.

THE POWER OF FICTIONAL SCENARIOS

Thomas Meyer, a University of Colorado professor who organized the "Case for Mars" series of conferences in the 1990s, shared some really interesting insights on the success of the space program during the 1960s. The race to the moon is hailed as not only the greatest technical accomplishment of mankind, but also as the quintessential team effort, comprising many players from throughout industry and academia who teamed up to defy seemingly impossible odds and beat the deadline of getting a man on the moon and safely back before the 1970s.

The German team led by Dr. Wernher von Braun in Huntsville, Alabama, was responsible for the development of the rockets that took the Apollo astronauts to the Moon, but those rockets would not have lifted an inch off the ground if it had not been for the extensive public support for the initiative. And, despite what many historians decry as a heavily politically tainted Cold War agenda being the real driver for the space program, the reason for the massive acceptance by the public of the effort and the money spent on it was that, for many years prior, the public's imagination had been successfully captured by science fiction writers who had instilled a vision of adventure related to going into space.

Ray Bradbury, H. G. Wells, Jules Verne, and others built up public support for the space program by delivering the vision and describing the promise of space exploration so that, when technology was ripe, the generation that had to implement and support the initiative was ready to rise up to the challenge.

Education in the 21st century faces a similar challenge, in that a substantial group of thinkers, authors, and educators are all converging on a bold vision for a better future, but they are still lone voices in the dark. These visions are powerful, but for them to materialize, much more is needed in terms of public support. Implementation constraints are the slow death of reform, and the only way to bridge the gap is, paradoxically, probably through fiction. Fiction liberates us from budgets, transition processes, test scores, and the litany of issues that can be roadblocks in the way of change. If I were granted one wish for education, it would be that somebody would write the *Harry Potter* of 21st-century education. What education needs right now, at this crossroads in history, is for some fictional scenario to capture people's minds and imaginations so that reform attempts resonate and find support with the general public. A Harry Potter–like blockbuster series of novels that depict the many benefits of customized education in the age of lifelong learning in a fun way would do wonders for advancing the 21st-century education cause.

A small measure of this is the recent success of Sir Ken Robinson as a speaker. I get frequent e-mails from people who call out to my attention the various lectures by Sir Ken that exist on the Web and that have been viewed by tens of millions of people. And the reason for his viral popularity is not just that the message he delivers really echoes with most people's perceptions of what is wrong and what schools are lacking, but also his delivery. His impeccable stand-up comedy timing and dry wit render Sir Ken as an irresistible attraction to people beyond the realm of education, inspiring them, as science fiction writers inspired people in the 1960s, to reach for the moon.

IMAGINING THE SCHOOL OF THE FUTURE

In the 21st-century visioning workshops that I run for educators to try to engender a collective 21st-century vision for their schools or districts, I challenge them to role-play the school of the future. Participants are charged with preparing a short sketch that depicts, in a few minutes, a learning situation in the school of the future, defined as the school at a time far enough ahead that implementation barriers are not considered.

It is always surprising and refreshing to see how, when placed in a constraint-free context, many educators who otherwise do not come across as overtly creative really get going and come up with many original ideas, most of them in sync with the basic premises of 21st-century education. The problem is that, despite getting it right in the fictional scenario, these same teachers and administrators falter in real life, and are clueless about how to bring forth the changes that they advocate in the safe, playful role-playing environment.

So, if we define the future, not in terms of a certain number of years ahead, but rather as the period in time in which foreseeable technology is mature enough to take definitive root in schools, and when implementation constraints have been removed, what will the school of the future be like?

Of course, there is no single right answer, and we don't know what the future will hold, but the exercise is still quite fruitful in stimulating thinking outside the box, and is a good first step to identifying the problems with the current system, and considering how to go about gradually jump-starting a change process.

Here are some of the possible characteristics of schools in the future. These are only *possible* developments, and the years to come may bring more changes, more advanced technological developments, and newer paradigms, but they offer a vague vision of what school could be like in the future.

Use of Virtual Reality and Educational Simulations

When (not if) technological progress allows for affordable delivery of realistic 3D, interactive, virtual reality (VR) environments, and when (and if) software developers invest in producing related educational applications and games that allow learners to immerse themselves in multisensory simulations, relevant learning will occur mostly through virtual reality.

After all, the transmission of knowledge, orally and in writing, is necessary because students cannot go through the experience itself, either because of physical impossibility (e.g., history) or because of the risk involved for novices (e.g., space exploration). As technological developments increasingly blur the limits between real life and simulated experiences, it makes a whole lot of sense to have students don their VR gear and start engaging in interactive, cooperative virtual reality learning experiences.

The possibilities are truly mind-blowing: students could participate in field trips, adventures, and reenactments of historic events; they could manage power plants, and conduct experiments; in a VR world, they could do anything that can be imagined. Instructors, coaches, or facilitators would become online guides and oversee the virtual environment to ensure, as they would in the physical world, that the excursion takes place without incident and within the established rules.

In this case, it is important not to create couch potato creatures that are incapable of physically doing anything, and these experiences should not mean the end of real physical experiments in laboratories, field trips, and so forth. Inversely, that concern should not negate the possibility of transporting students to simulated environments where they can replicate relevant experiences with great fidelity.

Physical Role of Schools

There is a question that looms large whenever schools of the future are discussed: what will actually take place in the schools themselves? It can easily be conceived that students do not actually need to be physically present within a school building and move around in a classroom with their virtual reality gear on; they could do that from their homes.

Arguments against this remote-controlled educational model spring up immediately, mostly having to do with the risks associated with a lack of social interactions between learners. However, that premise (or prejudice) is partly due to the mostly text-based mode of communication provided by computers today. Detractors say that communication itself is hindered by not being physically next to the person with whom you are communicating. In a future in which people can communicate fully with their counterparts through cyberspace, including virtual sensory experiences like touching, virtual reality communication may become almost indistinguishable from face-to-face communication.

Thinking about a full-blown cyber means of expression can be quite uncomfortable, and brings to mind some doomsday science fiction scenarios associated with the dehumanization of the human race. But, on the other hand, the virtual world and the possibility of creating an online avatar may very well free many kids from the harsh limitations of the real world. All educators have painfully witnessed the irreparable damage done to many children's self-esteem because of some physical characteristic that renders them undesirable or "not in" in the harsh and often cruel world of kids and adolescents.

There is no real dichotomy between physical interaction and learning, and the alarm bells that may ring in terms of the developing of social skills in a virtual world are justified and must be addressed. The possible dual personality individuals might develop between the real and online worlds, some sort of "cyber schizophrenia," is already an issue. Many educators have seen students become different people online from who they are in the physical world and they are baffled by this transformation—an apparent personality split between students' online and real-world personas. The real challenge is not to figure out how to do without social interactions, but rather how to rethink schools to enable them to engage students in these specially designed instances of social and physical interaction in a way that helps them develop the skills that are needed.

We may see a reduced number of hours a day in school that focus on mandatory activities for graduation, including physical education, games, creativity exercises, field trips, laboratory experiments, and other activities, while academic learning is conducted, synchronously or asynchronously, from the comfort and safety of home.

Teachers and Learners

A feature of the new school that even the teachers themselves are not afraid to enact is the fact that the traditional teacher role of "delivery from the pulpit" will definitely disappear. Never once during hundreds of 21st-century school role-playing sessions that I have witnessed have teachers gone back up to the front of a classroom and lectured. At most, their role is to guide, point to activities, and evaluate performance, but never ever to resume the current "sage on the stage" role.

In some cases, the roles of teacher and learner are not clearly delimited, and students take control of their own learning or become the group leaders for certain parts of the day or for certain activities. Even though this approach seems to be radically constructivist, the concept of the teacher being a learner with the students is a key component of the 21st-century paradigm, and is a strong indicator of how learning will be approached in the future.

Globally Interconnected

One of the most visible manifestations of the change in the general paradigm brought forth by the explosive growth in networking capabilities is the fact that we now live in a globalized, interconnected world that operates 24 hours a day, seven days a week. The most hyped and analyzed consequence of the globalized world is related to the workplace—outsourcing and global competitiveness—but there are challenges to education that go beyond preparing students to contend with a leveled playing field. Like never before, young people are exposed to an overwhelming and confusing multiplicity of stimuli at an age when the development of personality is strongly determined. Schools will need to embrace globalization as an integral part of the curriculum.

We can expect to see regular interactions with schools from other parts of the world. Projects in which students from a U.S. school in Iowa are paired up with students from Singapore and Brazil will be a daily occurrence in schools, with students in the group being assessed jointly. Data collection from each locale and information related to that particular culture will form part of the exchange, and will be jointly analyzed so as to reinforce the mantra "think globally and act locally."

State-of-the-art technology will naturally be used by students so that they can communicate and interact with each other, breaking down the existing physical distances, and a cultural component will probably be included in every project, so that the objective of learning to live together and value and appreciate different cultures is met.

Ubiquitous Learning

The "cells and bells" structural model is outdated, and the general landscape of how learning occurs in schools will radically change. The evolution in functionality and affordability of mobile technology will allow for learning to take place anywhere, so we can foresee schools resembling children's museums, with interactive exhibits and specifically designated areas that foster different kinds and levels of learning.

Simulation labs, science labs, outdoor activities and nature trails, workshops, and any other spaces that are conceived with a flexible and yet specific use in mind will host the physical learning experiences that actually take place in schools.

Flexible Scheduling

Fixed schedules that feature the same timetable for all children in school are a seemingly immovable constraint in the current school environment.

The future will allow each student, or at least each learning group, to have an individualized schedule to pursue learning objectives and manage time in a much more flexible way. The demise of the rigorously timed scheduling of lessons and adoption of a more flexible schedule will undoubtedly pose a challenge to administrators in charge of drawing up schedules, but hopefully related software will also have improved and will make the task more manageable.

Customized Learning

One of the greatest revolutions in 21st-century education will be that each and every student can learn to his or her own talents and learning styles. The school of the future will most definitely abandon the standard one-size-fits-all curriculum, and will be based on an individualized, customized program of study specifically designed to better suit the needs and developmental abilities of every learner.

Computer-based ongoing diagnostic assessments will keep track of the progress and development of each child, so we will be able to gauge and adjust what is best for each learner. The key role will be that of a "learning counselor," who will be in charge of determining the activities, projects, and learning activities that each student should engage in. As students progress in school and become older, they will increasingly have their own say about the direction of their individualized curriculum, based on their preferences and interests.

Graduation requirements may be made up of a set of competencies, abilities, and core content that need to be mastered, but the order, sequence, and correlativity of those areas, as well as an extensive menu of other optional curricular and cocurricular areas, will have a more substantial weight in schooling itself.

A Completely New Curriculum

In addition to being customized for each student, the curriculum in the school of the future will not look at all like the current heavily standardized curriculum that has an emphasis on certain content areas.

The curriculum in the school of the future will have a wider series of options for the students, and will include modular optional components that allow students to engage more in arts and other creative activities, not only with the current view of developing aesthetic appreciation and as a means of expression, which will continue to be important, but also with the goal of utilizing those activities as a catalyst for the development of higher-order thinking skills. Relatively recently, courses on right-brain drawing have become popular among corporate executives seeking to develop a more holistic ability to interpret ever-so-complex reality. We can expect that many such practices that delve into the creative arts as a source for the development of skills will find their way into the schools of the future.

Brain-Based Learning

Despite some conflicting reports from researchers on the effectiveness of the nascent learning applications of brain research, eventually, advances in our understanding about the inner workings of the brain will yield conclusions that will serve to enhance the learning process, to the benefit of all learners.

Coupled with powerful computerized periodic diagnostic tools that will monitor progress and development, the possibilities of brain-based learning are mind-boggling. Current research results in enormous benefits for students with learning difficulties, and what is known about the brain has generated many successful remedial practices. Brain-based research will eventually allow each learner to develop a full set of capabilities, resulting in an almost science-fiction scenario of increased intelligence for all learners. In his fascinating book *Disrupting Class: How Disruptive Innovation Will Change the Way the World Learns* (2008), innovation guru Clayton Christensen illustrates the point when he says, "Here is the dilemma: because students have different types of intelligence, learning styles, varying paces, and starting points, all students have special learning needs."

With early stimulation to help foster the development of certain abilities, the possibilities are endless. Brain-based learning may very well hold the key to finally constructing a better society.

Open View of Intelligence

A seemingly small issue, but one that is absolutely fundamental to truly building a new educational system, is our view of intelligence. Carol Dweck's seminal work on going beyond a rigid definition of intelligence, and her research on the positive influence of embracing an open mindset about intelligence—a belief that intelligence and talent are not fixed, and that they can grow throughout your life—have brought to the surface what good educators have known forever, that students respond to what teachers expect of them, and that, sadly, many learners have fallen victim to prejudice and low expectations from their teachers. Carol Dweck's book *Mindset: The New Psychology of Success* (2006), which presents compelling evidence that substantiates the hypothesis that intelligence is not limited, and that adopting the mindset that intelligence can grow has proven benefits, should be mandatory reading for all educators.

In the school of the future, intelligence or IQ tests will be regarded as laughable anachronisms, and mental fitness exercises, devoid of the quasi-derogatory connotations that they have today because research on that topic is still in its infancy, will become the norm in the same way that physical education targets body fitness and well-being.

Foreign Languages

It is almost a given that a greater focus on multiculturalism will result in the need to learn foreign languages, primarily as a way to be able to communicate with people from other cultures and benefit from interacting with people from those cultures via the Web. And the increased ease of traveling allows people to move around more than in the past. And there are other possible benefits of learning foreign languages. Many adults today were mercilessly subjected to years of Greek or Latin to help them develop structured thinking and logical abilities. As more knowledge is gained on the inner workings of the brain and the acquisition of certain skills, the learning of foreign languages can be put to some specific uses focusing on the capacities that doing so can help awaken. In a talk shown on the Fora.tv Web site, design thinking expert George Kembel relates how many Chinese children, because of their early exposure to Mandarin, a tonal language, have what musicians call perfect pitch, and as such would be able to identify spot-on any musical note that was being played. Not all Chinese students end up being gifted musicians, but the story illustrates that there is much we still do not know, and how our limited focus on the way we do things prevents us from making certain connections. In this case, for example, it would be interesting to research whether students who want to become gifted in music should learn Mandarin at a very age, both to pave the way for the development of a capacity that will serve them well in their chosen area of interest as well as to master a language whose importance in the evolving world is unquestionable.

Cooperation as the De Facto Standard

Most of the work done in the school of the future would not be individual, and students would participate in various different groups throughout their course of studies. As cooperative learning truly becomes the norm, more rigorous protocols will be developed to ascertain that the learning outcomes for all students allow them to contribute according to their learning styles and abilities, and also that they are "forced" to perform tasks and roles that may not be related to their dominant ability as a part of their learning process.

Learning by Doing

Regardless of the actual incarnation, whether it ends up being project-based learning, or problem-based learning, or any other type of learning by doing, the current predominant model of theoretical instruction with, at the most, a few exercises that partially exemplify and attempt to mirror reality, will be completely overtaken by a model that allows students to learn through hands-on participation in real-life projects, or solving real-life problems.

The traditional sequence of instruction that entails learning thoroughly before being allowed to actually do anything was rooted in the fact that knowledge needed to be acquired and stored so that it could be referenced in the future in order to be able to execute a task at a certain level of proficiency. The new environment, in which knowledge is infinitely accessible, has rendered that learning modality unnecessary. With a few exceptions in certain subject areas in which complexity still necessitates a broken-down sequential construction of knowledge, students can learn as they produce and perform, especially if they are using a simulated environment that neutralizes the risks and costs associated with mistakes.

Authors Bernie Trilling and Charles Fadel stress this in their book *21st Century Skills: Learning for Life in Our Times* (2009): "Recent research in cognition, the science of thinking, has punctured a time-honored tenet of teaching: that mastering contents must precede putting them to good use."

With the guidance of teacher-mentors or facilitators, students will spend a considerable amount of their time pondering, creating, analyzing, designing, and learning 21st-century skills by working on some complex real-life task that spans multiple disciplines. Working on projects or problems not only helps to develop certain higher-order skills, it also provides students with the chance to interact with experts from the outside world, helping to bridge the void between school and reality.

Environmental Stewardship

Fortunately, there is increased awareness of the need to preserve natural resources and to make responsible use of them. Environmental education will be at the heart of the school of the future, and as energy efficient systems, solar energy collecting and use, and water recycling methods become more economically viable and a common feature in schools, it will be essential to have students play an active role in the environmental policies of the school.

This concept of environmental stewardship that must be deeply ingrained in students from a very early age will result in students becoming actively involved with green roofs, orchards, and other hands-on ecological activities. And as they progress in knowledge it is quite conceivable that students will work on the building's environmental controls so that learners can play a formal role in the air conditioning, water recycling, solar energy storage and use, waste recycling, and other green features of the school building.

Higher-Order Skills Activities

The teaching of higher-order skills, such as creativity, critical thinking, analysis, inference, and the new needed skills that will evolve with the 21st century's fast-paced changes, will be addressed by means of specific spaces and activities intentionally designed to target each skill. Subject areas will be analyzed to see how each of them lends itself to the learning of these higher-order skills, and these skills will be learned transversely through the curriculum. Practices that are becoming increasingly frequent in the corporate environment, such as creative workshops, team building, and motivational sessions, will also become mainstream activities in schools.

Imagination and creativity are seriously endangered by a scenario that does not require us to visualize or invent anything and, as such, need to have their own specific space in the curriculum.

Excessive reliance on outside sources can also stifle students' abilities to assess, evaluate, measure, and infer, so we can imagine some sort of "intellectual survivor" session where students are faced with problems that have to be solved in a "clean room" environment, without accessing the Internet or any external resources.

These periodic exercises can also include students having to solve problems based on topics that they have never learned before (in this case, the exercise would foster students' capacity to effectively use Internet-based resources). As the years go by and students progressively hone their lifelong learning skills, these bare-bones challenges will be a great way to test their ability to work as a group and learn about new things on their own. This could be the closest thing to standardized assessment that exists in the future.

Interdisciplinary Learning

The heavily compartmentalized, artificial division of learning into subjects that now dominates curricula everywhere will gradually yield to transdisciplinary activities that span several subjects. In the school of the future, the structural unit of learning will not be the subject, but in all probability, the project, which will span the content and skills needed by each student as per their customized curriculum.

Teachers will, in all likelihood, not be subject teachers, but specialists in learning techniques and skill development, with a greater focus on cognition than on subject-matter expertise. Since lifelong learning will be the ultimate goal and the main driver, teachers who embody this learning mindset will be the ones who truly inspire the next generation of learners. We may see the idea of the generalist grade-level teacher extending into the older grades, and subject-matter specialists will be reserved to coach, mentor, and guide students in the more advanced courses (centered on projects).

No Textbooks

It is likely that in the future, textbooks will no longer exist, and their demise may occur sooner than we anticipate. Via mobile miniaturized devices or full laptops, students will access e-books as well as multimedia content that will completely replace textbooks. The whole concept of a textbook may be doomed, and even though fiction writing will probably still remain as a viable model, reference books will lose their identity and lose the battle to multimedia-based references.

Informal Learning

The importance of the informal learning occurring in schools, in many cases through extracurricular activities, will be acknowledged in the school of the future.

As we move towards recognizing that not all learning takes place strictly within academic subjects or in a formal regulated environment, the contribution of other activities and impromptu informal learning opportunities will gain relevance and become not accidental but intentional in the design of the school of the future.

In the workplace, because companies are only subjected to their own rules regarding training their employees and are not bound by any outside structural constraints, the value of informal learning is increasingly recognized as essential to the development of the workforce. Jay Cross (2006) vividly describes the importance of informal learning: "Workers learn more in the coffee room than in the classroom. They discover how to do their jobs through informal learning: talking, observing others, trial-and-error, and simply working with people in the know. Formal learning—classes and workshops—is the source of only 10 to 20 percent of what people learn at work."

The trend in the business world to underscore the importance of informal learning is consistent with the educational scenarios previously outlined: hands-on multidisciplinary projects where students mostly learn by doing are a way to learn from good practitioners, and their success provides a powerful illustration of the limitations of formal learning.

Robots

I have marginally alluded to a few science-fiction-type scenarios in the preceding paragraphs, but the possible uses of robots in school could be taken directly out of a futuristic movie. Nonetheless, it is no less plausible than many of the other developments envisioned for the school of the future.

Advances in the development of humanoid robots with increased artificial intelligence capabilities are bringing us closer to singularity, the point at which artificial intelligence surpasses human intelligence. Coupling advanced robots with human learning holds enormous promise to boost and enhance the learning experience.

Will robots become teaching assistants in the future? As spooky as that may sound, it is highly likely that advanced humanoid robots will become powerful aides in the learning process. But even if that were not the case, powerful software-based artificially intelligent educational packages will surely become invaluable tools for learning, not only in searching for or processing information, but also in data mining, analyzing and inferring, detecting trends over large data sets, and a whole series of other advanced thought processes that will supplement human intelligence.

Accreditation and Recognition of Schools

The customized and flexible school of the future with its promise of individualized learning is undoubtedly attractive and resonates with what we know to be right for the students. However, even as we acknowledge the benefits of a more flexible system that caters to each learner, validating schooling in that context may prove to be quite a difficult task.

In the context of a completely new educational paradigm that prioritizes individualized learning and lifelong learning and focuses much more on skills and abilities than content, the whole notion of accreditation, validation, or even standards needs to be viewed from a radically different perspective.

What would be the point of accrediting a school or defining standards when the basic premise of schooling is not centered on content? In the school of the future, students will, at different stages in the educational cycle, need to master certain primary competencies and skills and demonstrate knowledge of certain core content that is deemed necessary for them to be fully functional citizens.

Nobody can develop higher-order thinking skills about what is not known, and despite the infinite repository of online knowledge that has become ubiquitous, we do not want students to lose all their knowledge as soon as their Internet connection is switched off.

Defining a threshold level of knowledge, and even memorization, is a complex challenge that needs to be addressed, and should be the focus of concerted research efforts at local, national, and international levels.

Within that framework, a road map of tasks can be created that need to be accomplished by each learner, demonstrative of their abilities and skills as defined both locally and globally. Students need not necessarily comply with these tasks in a set order, but the planning of each learner's curriculum, activities, and projects should ensure that standards in terms of skills and content are met.

School graduation diplomas could then mark each learner's own journey of success, highlighting the tasks that were accomplished, as well as the level of proficiency attained in them.

ASSESSMENT IN THE SCHOOL OF THE FUTURE

I have deliberately left assessment as the final point to be analyzed, so as to look at it in the context of the preceding vision for the school of the future. The characteristics of the new school pose a stern challenge for assessment, one that defies what we take for granted in terms of evaluating students, and this, in turn, points us towards redefining the whole objective of assessment in the new paradigm.

The main driver behind assessment is evaluating whether students have acquired the desired knowledge and skills as per existing standards. However, in real life in schools, summative evaluations, which are by far still the norm, also provide "coercive motivation" that forces students to study and learn so as to obtain a passing grade that will allow them to make their way through the system.

The current assessment method is based on uniform expectations and heavily standardized exams, including the universally vilified high-stakes testing.

When we envision the school of the future, it becomes evident that the current prevailing model of assessment would be completely inadequate. It is unfathomable to imagine a customized, personalized curriculum that caters to each individual with progress and goal attainment measured by sit-down written examinations that are administered concurrently and are the same for all students.

One key element is that assessment will finally be heavily weighted towards being formative rather than summative—it will be an integral part of the learning process. Written end-of-unit tests, high-stakes end-of-course evaluations, and other summative incarnations of the industrialized model of assessment will be gradually phased out.

Evaluation of students will be more focused on skills than content, and will be continuous, implicit, diversified, will focus on the process more than the final product, and will allow for mistakes to occur as part of the learning process.

Profound reform is needed, because the conventional focus on factual recall and memorization is rendered useless in an era of continuously available information. Assessment systems will need to focus on the development of higher-order skills, and these skills must be demonstrated through the completion of related complex tasks.

A good example of how these objectives may be achieved is the "rich tasks" that are at the core of the curriculum in the Australian province of Queensland. An initiative of Education Queensland that applies to all schools in that Australian province, rich tasks are systematically interspersed throughout the curriculum. They are a series of transdisciplinary tasks that constitute "a reconceptualization of the notion of outcome as demonstration or display of mastery; that is, students display their understanding, knowledge and skills through performance on transdisciplinary activities that have an obvious connection to the wide world" (www.education.qld.gov.au).

It can't be stressed enough how important it will be to redefine the scope and focus of assessment to encompass significant learning in the context of the 21st-century paradigm. A few years back, there was a global contest organized by a school challenging students to find, as fast as possible, answers to more than 200 trivia questions (each participating school submitted questions). Teams of power Googlers were organized to find the right answers in the least possible time, and students came up with more than 200 right answers to factual questions in no time. But did they actually learn anything? This example of how the use of a technological tool may yield the desired outcome and yet not constitute any significant learning (the activity was designed to measure what is not necessarily relevant—it measured the correctness of the answers and the time it took to get them, but not how they were attained) is a harsh reminder of the need to completely redefine assessment.

What will assessment look like in the school of the future, since at first glance it seems to require a teacher-to-student ratio that is impossible from an operational point of view?

The change in the learning process is defining of new forms of assessment, since learning will not occur in the adult-led, student-passive model but rather with the student becoming actively engaged in learning. A greater emphasis on hands-on projects invalidates any form of assessment that is not formative and conducive to acquiring incremental mastery of the task at hand. The changed role of teachers to that of coaches or mentors also facilitates a transition towards providing real-time relevant feedback.

Paradoxically, assessment in the future will more closely resemble what goes on in a sports game than what currently takes place inside a classroom. Coaches give feedback in the locker room after the game, mostly with a view to improve performance in the next outing. But out on the field, the players are focused on playing the game, and during the game itself, the coach on the sideline is providing instantaneous feedback on performance to correct whatever behavior is hindering the team's success.

Technology can come to the rescue when it comes to assessment. We can expect students to be assessed by means of digital portfolios that document stages in the learning process, game logs that record the achievement of objectives in the game, computer adaptive testing that generates questions based on continuous diagnosis of the learner's abilities, and many other developments that can help and enhance the learning process. The gaming metaphor is especially adequate, since mistakes are not penalized, and games have unlimited tries, successive stages that add levels of difficulty, and feedback that is instantaneous and constructive.

The use of virtual reality and simulations will also allow participants to collectively complete objectives, set up and accomplish missions, and so forth. Computer programs that will keep a log of all of these activities, including individual contributions, will provide a great starting point for post-session debriefings that can constitute valuable learning experiences. In the space program, astronauts recall that after grueling simulations, the debriefing sessions with the simulations team in which both astronauts and mission controllers reviewed performances were the best learning experiences, and helped to blend the team as well.

The flip side of this coin is that, as wonderful as it may be that instructors can check digital logs to review learner progress, there are ethical concerns that the individual learning history of students may eventually be used against them, with errors or difficulties at a very early age being brought to the surface out of context many years later when, for example, prospective employers demand that information.

Because of the extent of its disconnect with the new paradigm, assessment is a good starting point for reform, and we can expect to see some of these changes as pioneer efforts in the development of the school of the future.

THE FUTURE OF SCHOOLS

Although it is a fascinating exercise, it is hard to predict what the school of the future will look like, and what exactly will happen in a future that, by definition, is unknown. So this attempt at envisioning the school of the future should not be taken as a prediction, or even necessarily as a recommendation for what schools in the future should be like.

More important than whatever pedagogical incarnation we end up with are the underlying principles of personalization, catering to each and every learner's needs, the prime goal of lifelong learning, and an instructional process more centered on the learner than the teacher.

In *Catching Up or Leading the Way: American Education in the Age of Globalization* (2009), author Yong Zhao eloquently summarizes these trends:

> A truly global mindset about education suggests that tolerance for multiple perspectives, different talents and a respect for diversity are key to a brighter future for all. As we enter a new era in human history, we cannot be certain of what specific talents, knowledge and skills will be of value, and globalization has expanded the market; therefore, we must accept the idea that all talents, all individuals are worthwhile. Education is thus intended to help every child realize his or her potential. Every child counts!

In its document entitled *A National Conversation about Personalised Learning* (2004), the United Kingdom Department for Education makes a strong and clear statement in favor of a customized and personalized education for the future:

> To build a successful system of personalized learning, we must begin by acknowledging that giving every single child the chance to be the best they can be, whatever their talent or background, is not the betrayal of excellence, it is the fulfillment of it. Personalized learning means high-quality teaching that is responsive to the different ways students achieve their best. There is a clear moral and educational case for pursuing this approach. A system that responds to individual pupils, by creating an education path that takes account of their needs, interests and aspirations, will not only generate excellence, it will also make a strong contribution to equity and social justice.

We are the generation that will have to ride out this perfect educational storm, but once we emerge out of it, there is no doubt in my mind that the future of schools will be better, and that the schools of the future will be better schools, schools that will serve our students and their families, and that will ultimately help build a better future for everyone.

CHAPTER TEN

Models for the
School of the Future

BY AINSLEY ROSE

"THE COMPLEXITY OF TEACHING is beyond the complexity of being Monet or Emily Carr. It is the artful integration of the science in teaching. It is about getting better, it is about being wiser, it is about making a difference" (Bennett and Rolheiser, 2001).

It seems more than apparent, given the litany of articles, books, blogs, newspaper accounts, and other media publications, that the impact of the 21st century has captured imaginations and generated substantive intrigue in a variety of areas, not the least of which is the arena of education. Whether it is the use of technology and its impact on teaching, or the speed at which present textbooks are becoming irrelevant, or the ubiquity of computers, or the need to promote a greater emphasis on creativity and critical thinking, educators are yet again being held to account.

This chapter will address only a few of the challenges that schools in the future will face. Our work only has meaning in the application of the ideas we have taken pains to outline up to this point. What we need now is to suggest what educators can do to implement some strategies in their schools to make these ideas come alive. In other words, we need to make the future materialize with form, substance, and shape rather than just an ethereal dream on a page, or in cyberspace. The key is to understand to what extent the challenge is one of instruction, organization of schools, or the need to completely shift the paradigm of school.

Despite the intriguing quote above, 21st-century instruction requires a shift in approach from our current model of a teacher-initiated, teacher-driven paradigm to one of a student-centric, learner-involvement approach. Davidson and Goldberg (2009) introduce the notion of participatory learning. As they put it, "participatory learning includes the many ways that learners (of any age) use new technologies to participate in virtual communities where they share ideas, comment on one another's projects, and plan, design, implement, advance, or simply discuss their practices, goals, and ideas together." Clearly this suggests a move away from the teacher as the "sage on the stage" to a position of the teacher as the "guide on the side." Students will be expected to become partners in the learning-teaching process rather than the object of attention and passive recipients of instruction emanating strictly from the teacher as the sole provider of the content. Trilling and Fadel (2009) have created a chart (see Figure 2) to demonstrate the clear differences between our present model of teaching and learning compared to the desired model of learning and teaching in 21st-century classrooms. The "Learning Balance Chart," as they refer to it, makes the distinctions quite clear.

The "Learning Balance Chart" and other models show very adequately how learning should be shifted towards a new model. However, the general mindset for implementation is often mutually exclusive. Either schools will need to be this or schools will need to be that. Schools need to have this curriculum or that curriculum. Jim Collins (2001) suggests that we need to embrace the notion of "both and" as a framework for reform. As the saying goes, we do not want to throw out the baby with the bath water. In her speeches, education consultant Carol Commodore puts it this way: "What we know today does not make yesterday wrong, it makes tomorrow better." There is much we should retain, in the same way that the medical profession should consider the risk of eliminating effective procedures, surgeries, and treatments just because they are "old."

Whether one thinks about this century or the previous one, the success of all schools rests in the hands of the teachers, in particular through the instruction they deliver on a daily basis. However, given what Bennett and Rolheiser state above, whether it is art or science,

FIGURE 2	Learning Balance Chart	
Current model	**Desired model**
Teacher-directed	Learner-centered
Direct instruction	Interactive exchange
Knowledge	Skills
Content	Process
Basic skills	Applied skills
Facts and principles	Questions and problems
Theory	Practice
Curriculum	Projects
Time-slotted	On-demand
One-size-fits-all	Personalized
Competitive	Collaborative
Classroom	Global community
Summative tests	Formative evaluations
Text-based	Web-based
Learning for school	Learning for life

effective teaching remains an elusive dream in many of our current classrooms. Marzano (2007) says, "Among elements such as a well-articulated curriculum and a safe and orderly environment, the one factor that surfaced as the single most influential component of an effective school is the individual teachers within that school." This underscores the importance of what the teacher actually does with the instruction they dispense, regardless of other factors. Marzano (2007) points out that while the teacher is critical, whether teaching is an art or a science, it remains that there is no single formula for effective teaching. There is no one most effective way to teach. He notes, "research will never be able to identify instructional strategies that work with every student in every class. The best research can do is tell us which strategies have a good chance (i.e. high probability) of working well with students. Individual classroom teachers must determine which strategies to employ with the right student at the right time. In effect, a good part of effective teaching is an art. . . ."

While Hattie (2009) chooses to not make any distinction between the art and science of teaching as do Marzano (2007) and Bennett and Rolheiser (2001), Hattie does point out that what happens during the instruction in any given year is not as important as what happens when students react to what has been taught—in other words, "what happens next."

There is a never-ending drive to create powerful learning environments that require teachers to have knowledge of creative, intelligent instruction methods along with a deep understanding of their subject knowledge. Given the challenges of the 21st century, most of which are as yet unknown in terms of what will constitute the content and skills students will be expected to learn in this new century, what might be some of the necessary and essential elements of the instructional process that teachers will have to embrace in order to be effective?

We must examine the matter of teacher instruction and its evolution, as well as the complexity of the instructional process that makes effective teaching in all classrooms elusive for the future classroom and students' needs in the 21st century. The impact of recent cognitive research bears examination as it relates to our knowledge about how students learn and what we need to take into account as a result of this new and interesting research about the brain. While there is ample enthusiasm to embrace some applications that result from brain research in a real way, there is still doubt as to whether or not current brain research is substantive enough for real classroom application.

We also must consider other questions: Why are some teachers more effective than others when teaching the same students? What are some of the instructional decisions teachers need to consider that will consistently lead to greater gains in student achievement? To what degree does the involvement of students in the instructional process lead to more effective instruction? How does group work enhance the instructional process and what are the differences between cooperative learning and group work? What are some of the strategies, skills, and tactics that have a greater effect on student learning, and how can they be utilized in a greater number of schools and classrooms?

The challenge of teaching students in schools today seems to have resulted in greater levels of frustration for all. Teachers claim that students are arriving in their classes with ever-increasing disabilities, lower motivation, and less engagement when in school. Parent participation in their children's progress is becoming increasingly rare in some schools. Post-secondary institutions insist that students are arriving ill-prepared for their institutions. Business and industry claim that the applicants for job openings do not have the skills to complete job applications as a result of their poor literacy skills. International tests of achievement results show that students in the United States lag far behind students in other countries whose socioeconomic conditions are not as favorable as those in North America. Furthermore, Thomas Friedman (2007) points out that in developing countries such as India, the total number of advanced students is a larger number than all the students in all our schools in the United States. This serves to remind us of the globally competitive nature of the schooling dilemma.

Despite this glum litany of ills that plague our school systems, there remain pockets of excellence that defy the odds—outliers, as it were. What is it these schools are doing that has led to such success despite the sea of mediocrity in which they exist? How can these islands of good practice serve as pointers to initiate positive change? We do know that powerful teaching makes a difference. Linda Darling-Hammond (2008) identifies three things that need to be present for teaching to be effective:

> 1) Students come to the classroom with prior knowledge that must be addressed if teaching is to be effective. 2) Students need to organize and use knowledge conceptually if they are to apply it beyond the classroom. 3) Students learn

more effectively if they understand how they learn and how to manage their own learning.

This is what typifies the needs of the 21st-century learner: inquiry, problem solving, application, and production (Darling-Hammond, 2008). Although there is still no real agreement on what those skills really need to be or look like, there does appear to be some consensus among a wide range of authorities on this topic (Rose, 2010).

The other consideration is the litany of instructional approaches that have been developed over the years, each of which purports to be the best for students to learn the very skills that we now demand for 21st-century learners. There are several broad categories into which we can place these specific approaches. One such category is inquiry learning. Another is cooperative learning, and we could even suggest direct instruction approaches, among others.

STUDENT-CENTRIC APPROACHES FOR INSTRUCTION

In inquiry learning, one might include project-based, problem-based, and design-based approaches, all of which have similar attributes but differ in application (Darling-Hammond, 2008). Cooperative learning, on the other hand, could include collaborative strategies. Linda Darling-Hammond (2008) cites one particular approach, called collaborative reasoning, that can be included in this notion of collaborative (as distinct from cooperative) learning.

What I find interesting is that regardless of which instructional method one considers, in every case, it is up to the teacher to exercise the intelligence to use the method that is most suitable given the intersection of various essential factors: the student, the curriculum to be taught, and the strategy to be invoked so as to maximize learning. The complexity of this act, notwithstanding other considerations such as which assessment is to be used at what time under what conditions and for what purpose, further compounds the challenge.

More recently, research on the brain, made possible by fMRI imaging techniques, has introduced yet another element into the already challenging world of instruction and teaching. While there is great excitement about the developments in brain research and its application to education, it is still too early to tell if some of the claims being made by researchers will bring applications to the classroom that will lead to improvements in student achievement. Recall the excitement over the "Mozart effect," when researchers claimed that exposing children to the music of Mozart would lead to enhanced intellectual performance. However, it was determined that there is nothing to substantiate that such an effect exists, and that there is no real benefit, despite several attempts to replicate the findings of the original study. This led to the conclusion that "in general, applications of brain-based theories to education and assessment are relatively limited at this time, though that may not be the case in the future. As Bruer (1997, 1999) and others have noted, brain research by itself currently provides limited guidance for understanding or modifying complex higher-order cognitive processes" (National Research Council, 2001).

The German Research Ministry published a report in 2006 that summarized the findings of more than 300 articles about the relationship between music exposure and intelligence. It concluded that "... passively listening to Mozart—or indeed any other music you enjoy—does not make you smarter. But more studies should be done to find out whether music lessons could raise your child's IQ in the long term" (Abbot, 2007).

Other studies have come to the same conclusion. An account in *Nature* (www.nature.com) that has been called "the largest study of computerized brain-training activities to date" shows that although subjects' ability to perform a specific task increases, their performance on tests that measure things like memory and learning—general cognitive abilities—is not noticeably improved.

"There were absolutely no transfer effects," said lead author Adrian Owen, a neuroscientist at the Medical Research Council Cognition and Brain Sciences Unit in Cambridge, England. "I think the expectation that practicing a broad range of cognitive tasks to get yourself smarter is completely unsupported" (www.21stcenturythinker.com). It appears that the impact of Mozart's music on the learning of a newborn child is still inconclusive and warrants much further examination.

What this does confirm, however, is that there remains an abiding wish to find the "fountain of smart," the gold at the end of the rainbow, the magic elixir that will forever eradicate the idea that some children are not able to learn at high levels, and that will make all children able to accomplish things that heretofore are only pipe dreams for most.

While disappointing to some degree, what we do know is that brain research has helped educators understand some learning abnormalities and increasingly some of the causes of specific learning disorders. It seems that the most immediate application of this learning would be to help fulfill the need for differentiation of content, expectations, assessment, and curriculum for those students who struggle with the material and the style of teaching to which they are exposed.

Howard Gardner's (2006) "multiple intelligences" and Robert Sternberg's (1988) "triarchic theory of intelligence," among others, have helped us recognize the complexities of learning and therefore of teaching that must accompany all these factors in the classroom. One can appreciate the increasingly challenging role the teacher needs to fulfill in order to be effective.

CURRENT MODELS OF STUDENT-CENTRIC LEARNING

There are a variety of challenges for the classroom teacher, but there are also current examples where, despite these challenges, teachers are being effective and students are learning at high levels. Not only are there teachers experiencing success in teaching challenging students, but also there are schools that are making a difference in children's lives and education. The essence of these schools revolves around a socioconstructive approach based on the research of Russian psychologist Lev Vygotsky from the 1930s that is now taking its rightful place in the classroom (en.wikipedia.org). Some of the examples that follow are built on these notions of socioconstructivism. Vygotsky's other contributions to our understanding of child growth and learning include the zone of proximal development and self-regulation. All of these notions have influenced some the examples that follow, although not all consciously.

In Linda Darling-Hammond's interesting book *Powerful Learning* (2008), she cites several examples of schools that have embraced some of the instructional possibilities that are available and effective. One such example is that of the Expeditionary Learning Schools Outward Bound model. King Middle School, Casco Bay High School, and the Springfield Renaissance schools in Portland, Maine, have implemented this process with great documented success. The Bill and Melinda Gates Foundation financially supports some of these exemplary schools. Project-based learning schools can also showcase examples of the uses of this technique as the center of curriculum (Darling-Hammond, 2008). Co-nect schools have as their basis of instruction an emphasis on the use of technology combined with an instructional disposition to project-based learning. Teachers work in interdisciplinary teams in a collaborative culture. This combination is thought to elicit high levels of student engagement as well as a greater opportunity to develop a clear set of academic standards and alignment throughout a school. Co-nect is actually a service provider for schools that have as their core methodologies distributed educational leadership strategies, job-embedded learning, collaborative teacher study teams, and an emphasis on the use of data as a basis for planning and review. Some examples of these schools follow. Although not all are Co-nect schools, they could be, as their ideals bear a striking resemblance to those of Co-nect schools.

SCHOOL MODELS TO REPLICATE

The JASON Science Project has pioneered another marvelous example of innovative teaching. The project connects students with great explorers and great events to inspire and motivate them to learn science (www.jason.org).

Preschool and kindergarten children can also benefit from innovative approaches to learning environments. Take for example Blue School, whose mission statement reads, "Our mission is to cultivate creative, joyful and compassionate inquirers who use courageous and innovative thinking to build a harmonious and sustainable world" (www.theblueschool.org).

Here is the Blue School's approach to learning:

> Our educational model is made up of two components: the core curriculum, which represents the basic academic subjects our program will cover, and the values, which describe our approach and the key elements we want to "connect" to the subjects in our curriculum. Each of our values relates in some way to the idea of connection, whether it be the connection to a community, to one's emotions, to one's artistic voice, to one's body, to the world, to one's interests, or to one's sense of joy and wonder. Our model emerged out of a desire to achieve a new kind of balance between *academic rigor* and *academic enchantment.* We believe that both are essential attributes of a truly exceptional education. (www.theblueschool.org)

Interestingly, some universities, too, are taking advantage of our new understandings about the need to alter and rethink instructional models that can have great impact on student learning, and to institutionalize that thinking into practice with real students and then measure the effect and impact on student achievement and engagement. For example, Stanford University in Palo Alto, California, describes its instructional and curriculum approach in this manner: "Born out of a need to capture emerging technologies and use them to advantage by creating learning environments conducive for them, Stanford created courses specifically designed to maximize the utility of these emerging technologies" (www.standford.edu). The Stanford school is designed to bind the faculties of business, engineering, medicine, education, and the humanities with one focus to work together to solve big challenges in what they refer to as a human-centered way. The school's Learning, Design, and Technology (LDT) master's degree program uses methods from the various disciplines that make up its "d.School" (Institute of Design) and combines them to develop innovators rather than a particular innovation or product.

> The LDT experience is without equal. Students join a select cohort diverse in background and skills, thus enabling knowledge-sharing and cross-pollination of ideas. Under the guidance of an academic advisor, students align their program of study to their specific goals. Courses from practically every department at Stanford are open to LDT students, including those in design, engineering, business, fine arts, law, and of course, education. Combined with internships, team assignments, and a major project, LDT delivers an appropriate mix of theory and practice to help professionals achieve their full potential. (www.standford.edu)

It is one thing to talk of the instructional skills, strategies, and tactics we need to be mindful of in public schools. It is quite another to realize that the institutions that are producing our future teachers are able to make significant changes to their preservice programs in order to spawn a new generation of teachers who will be able to handle these new environments. Consider what the University of Washington teacher education program has attempted to do in recent years to meet the demand of new methodologies for our 21st-century learners. Their program includes engaging fieldwork, connecting practice with research, field-based instruction, and inquiry-based practice, among other considerations that are common to current teacher education programs. They specifically mention that their "programs reflect a strong orientation toward inquiry, both in the methods we promote among teachers and examinations of the effectiveness of our own work" (www.education.washington.edu).

Linda Darling-Hammond (2008) proposes that there is another instructional approach that comes from the notion that children learn at higher and deeper levels if they are asked to design and create articles that require them to think and apply their acquired knowledge.

Increasingly, it seems that the discipline of science is leading the way when it comes to innovation and change in how science is taught in schools. There are many examples of these innovative approaches across the country and, indeed, around the world. In the United States, the FIRST (For Inspiration and Recognition of Science and Technology) program stands out. Founded by inventor and scientist Dean Kamen, the vision of FIRST is "to transform our culture by creating a world where science and technology are celebrated and where young people dream of becoming science and technology leaders" (www.usfirst.org).

FIRST captures the spirit and intent of 21st-century instructional methodologies. They have coined two delicious terms that the education sector could well adopt, as these terms exemplify exactly what we should be trying to promote in our classrooms and schools in America. One term is "gracious professionalism™"; the other is "coopertition™." They say, "gracious professionals learn and compete like crazy, but treat one another with respect and kindness in the process." Coopertition is "displaying unqualified kindness and respect in the face of fierce competition. Coopertition is founded on the concept and a philosophy that teams can and should help and cooperate with each other even as they compete" (www.usfirst.org).

Each of these examples has been built around some of the principles and practices of the constructivist model made explicit by Lev Vygotsky (1962) and Jean Piaget (1998) in their early writings about learning and psychology. While there are many other models of teaching we could dwell on at length, there appears to be a growing consensus that a constructivist approach to teaching and learning offers our best hope of improving education in the 21st century.

Given the complexity of the enterprise of classroom instruction, it cannot be left to wishes, hopes, and dreams of a better future for education. Rather, we need to make a concerted effort to be consistent, persistent, and insistent that schools across the country pay heed to the body of knowledge that has emerged about learning. John Hattie, in *Visible Learning* (2009), cites the research that shows that the teacher in the classroom has the greatest impact on learning of all factors. By implication, what the teacher does by way of instruction plays a huge role in their impact and effectiveness on student learning now and in the future. But now and in the future, learning will need to revolve around notions such as student-centric instruction, collaborative approaches, student involvement, personalized learning or customized learning, lifelong learning, and problem-based or inquiry-based learning that encompasses the notions of big ideas and essential questions. This list is not exhaustive; it is a beginning list for schools to consider, explore, and develop in order to prepare for the dramatic changes in ideology about teaching and learning that the pressures of the 21st century demand.

STUCK IN THE PAST

While education's past structures and models must surely inform the future, we must be careful not to be limited by the thinking that led to some mistakes in those models and structures. The oft-repeated phrase "thinking outside the box" is appropriate here. It is novel, creative, maybe even outlandish thinking that is required to break the mold if we are ever to see new horizons in education. The instructional models cited above may well be the bridge we should use to cross over to a new vision of schooling.

Schools of all types—public, private, charter, universities, and other forms of schools—have fundamentally held to archaic modes of delivery despite repeated calls for change in structures, process, and content over the years. Despite all the reports, books, articles, white papers, and more on the subject, furor over how schools work, or do not work, remains high. Why is this the case? Countries, states, provinces, cities, and towns continue to preserve the institution of schools as they are currently constituted, while at the same time demanding that those schools improve the quality of education that they offer.

The No Child Left Behind Act in the United States has accelerated the problem despite the best of intentions. Its creators clearly hoped to raise the level of success of U.S. schools on international tests of achievement. It is interesting to note that the 2009 PISA (Programme for International Student Assessment) results show that the United States trails badly; some smaller countries who spend far less annually per student than the United States achieve better results overall (www.oecd.org). We add more evaluation of students, teachers, principals, and school districts; increase the levels and amount of standardized testing; threaten dire consequences for those schools that are not able to reach their AYP (adequate yearly progress) targets, and expect that all will be well—scores will rise, and teachers will be more satisfied. But despite having worked harder and longer, we have achieved less. Some schools have decided to provide incentives—pay teachers and administrators more when they do achieve higher results than the year before, thinking that the promise of more money will surely provide an incentive for principals and teachers to work with a greater sense of purpose and zeal. But, here, too, we have little to show for well-intentioned inducements. It appears that schools continue to flounder, students are still not engaged, and teachers and principals continue to be discouraged despite the care and attention given to making a difference.

When a business is floundering, it is left with difficult choices: declare bankruptcy, go though some process of renewal, or succumb to a takeover. So what of schools when they are in difficulty? As the saying goes, "If the horse is dead, dismount." In education, we say, "If the horse is dead, try to ride the dead horse," or we redefine the term "dead," or, as a colleague of mine says, we hire a consultant to teach us how to ride a dead horse.

Schools have not changed in organization (hierarchy), management (top-down), expectations (compulsory standards for all), approach (teacher holds all the information), duration (five days a week for 180 days in the United States, with four to six periods of 50 or so minutes) or requirements for successful passage to the next level, whether grade to grade or level of schooling (narrow and increasingly rigorous graduation requirements), so fewer students are able to graduate, and still the institutions that are receiving these students complain they are not ready. What are we to do? What are the solutions to this dilemma?

It was Einstein who said, "We can't solve problems by using the same kind of thinking that we used when we created them." Schools are trying to create new structures using the same old patterns and processes of schooling that have existed for the past 200 years. Life coach Anthony Robbins puts it this way: "If you always do what you have always done, you will always get what you always got."

Trying to accomplish new things with old methods "puts education and educators in the position of bringing up the rearguard, of holding desperately to the fragments of an educational system which, in its form, content, and assessments, is deeply rooted in an antiquated mode of learning" (www.futureofed.org).

Could it be that the basic premise of school change is what is really at fault? Is it that we see the symptoms, but are still unclear about the causes of this malaise in our schools? Here is what Cornelia Dean (2008) has to say about institutions of higher learning, which are even more ensconced in the old way of "doing school":

> Oxford University, the longest continuously running university in the English-speaking world, was founded in the twelfth century. Only the Catholic church has been around longer, and, like the Catholic church, universities today bear a striking structural resemblance to what they were in medieval times.

When one reads the litany of papers, books, and articles on 21st-century learning, one quickly comes to the conclusion that all we have to do to update our schools is to simply change the curriculum, or methods of assessment, or type of instruction, and we are off to the races. This "new" model is going to propel us into the 21st century, despite the fact that ten years of this new century have already passed us by.

The myth of school reform rests in the notion that changing the curriculum, or the nomenclature, or the subject matter, or purchasing a "new program," will guarantee an increase in achievement scores. Are higher scores all it would take to justify these solutions to what ails education, schools, and teaching? It is naïve, trite, and just a little insulting to all those who call themselves educators to suggest that the "fix" for schools is to merely tinker with what currently exists. We need to consider matters such as the disposition of learners towards what they are studying, the level of creativity we should be trying to cultivate, and the level of joy and satisfaction students get out of their efforts. As Carol Dweck suggests, we need to cultivate, in students and in ourselves, an open mindset about intelligence (Dweck, 2006).

More recently, we have embraced the latest in-vogue cure for all that ails us in education—technology. A significant part of this book makes the case for doing so. But while there is no doubt that technology will transform (and has already transformed) our schools in many ways, our reliance on computers and other technological innovations, while necessary, is not sufficient to make the real difference we are looking for. For one thing, schools and school districts cannot afford to keep up with the level and speed of innovation that technology generates. The shelf life of most technology is being reduced to months. Memory size, processing speed, touch screens, cell phones, bandwidth, video-conferencing, platforms, and software versions are changing at such a pace that schools are having trouble keeping up. Invariably, schools are at least one, if not more, generation of technology behind what the market is producing. While technology costs are being lowered, schools are still far from being able to purchase the necessary equipment for their students, particularly given the new programs' thirst for memory and processing power that most older machines can't handle.

The debate over wireless versus hardwired schools presents another challenge. Whether it is best to have one portable computer per child, or shared labs, is still debated in some quarters, although it might seem obvious that the old concept of the lab is outdated and outmoded. Can you picture teachers taking their classes to a central location to use an overhead projector or whiteboard, rather than having it in their respective classrooms? But many schools try to maximize the use of the few computers they are able to afford by placing them in centralized labs so that all students can have access to them, albeit on a limited basis. Christensen (2008) supports this practice when he states, "If the addition of computers to classrooms were a cure, there would be evidence of it by now. There is not. Test scores have barely budged. There must be a better explanation than more computers and technology."

The use of technology also results in a related problem: Many members of the latest generation of hardwired (or wireless) students arrive at school already more tech-savvy than the teachers who are expected to teach them. When schools inform their teachers that, effective next week, all the school announcements and memos will now be transmitted through e-mail, there is a collective gasp from the adults in the building who have managed to resist any technological intrusion into their professional lives. In those educators' defense, many schools do not offer their teachers training in computer literacy, and to make matters worse, technical support is often available on a very limited basis.

In order for technology to be embraced, school decision makers need to take ownership of the challenges that inevitably arise with the ever-increasing demands for implementation of sophisticated technology. It is vital that the advent of technological solutions be made possible, and not be subject to the usual vagaries of budgets, manpower, or expertise. Technology has the capability to provide educational environments for all types of learners, environments that may well solve the problems associated with instituting individualized instruction for all students. We most certainly need technology to serve us, and not the other way around.

School systems are notoriously good at maintaining the status quo. Parents call for a back-to-basics focus, with the thought that "it worked for us, surely it will work for our children." Politicians call for educational change in virtually every election. Often, for them, the "change" they seek in education is to get back to a system with which they are comfortable: grades, punishment, longer hours, more school days, and more frequent evaluation of the teachers and students. While their demands on our schools are justified, many decision makers are sadly mistaken in their beliefs about what will make a difference.

We know that students don't all learn the same way, nor do they all have the same levels of motivation or the support to learn at all, let alone at high levels, from their families. A key step in making school motivating is to tailor the learning to meet the needs of each child. But, as Christensen (2008) suggests, "Schools' interdependent architectures force them to standardize the way they teach and test. Standardization clashes with the need for customization in learning." He says that schools need to move away from a one-size-fits-all approach to a more "modular, student-centric approach, using software as an important delivery vehicle." Software can be the lifeblood for new and interesting strategies to reach those children that heretofore have been subjected to teaching methods that prevent them from moving beyond the low expectations that are set for them by teachers and that they set for themselves.

We do not need an evolution of our school system; we need a *revolution* of our school system.

Some question whether we need a school system at all. "Hole-in-the-wall" experiments conducted by an Indian researcher demonstrated that children who had little prior experience with technology were able to figure out and teach each other how to use computers, and without instruction, make computers do things that many adults are unable to make them do (www.ted.com).

VIRTUAL SCHOOLS

There are some schools that look nothing like our present conception of a school. You might ask, "Where are these schools, and how can I have my child attend such an institution?" You have already presumed that these schools consist of a building in a specific location housing children. That is our current way of thinking. "Outside-the-box" thinking is what is needed to conceive of other possibilities.

There are presently a variety of organizations that we might want to call schools, but which don't look anything like or even act like our current conception of "schools." There are pioneering souls out there who have the courage and the inclination to create new ways of learning. Some of their ideas have already been made into reality, and they are demonstrating that there are other ways for students to learn, and to do so at high levels and with increasing levels of commitment and engagement.

Some great work has been done to rethink what schools of the future need to be. By "school" I do not mean a building with classrooms built to house a certain number of students, built according to government specifications on what the square footage funding formulas say you are entitled to based on demographic projections for the next 25 years.

Many of these organizations or initiatives begin with a clear commitment to the foundational principles and values around which all their thinking, planning, and creation revolve. They serve as a model of the thinking that they wish to promote; this is the way schools should be conceived. They have fundamentally rethought the concepts of "school" and "schooling" by reconstructing all aspects of our current and outmoded model. A report by Davidson and Goldberg (2009) entitled "The Future of Learning Institutions in a Digital Age" says, "We contend that the future of learning institutions *demands* a deep, epistemological appreciation of the profundity of what the Internet offers humanity as a model of a learning institution."

The report goes on to say, "A *New York Times* article from 2008 even suggested that a future Nobel Prize winner might not be an oncology researcher at a distinguished university, but a blogging community where multiple authors, some with no official form of expertise, actually discover a cure for a form of cancer through their collaborative process of combining, probing, and developing insights online together."

Clearly, the notion of virtual learning is one such innovation that conceives of a school, not as a building, but rather as a location to which a variety of people can go to collaborate. Wikipedia, reputed to be the largest encyclopedia compiled in human history, written collaboratively by people around the world, most of whom have never met each other, is one such example of what is possible.

Our current structures and institutions must clearly reinvent themselves in forms that take into account the ubiquity of the tools and resources that pervade our present existence. Digital tools will continue to shape all our institutions, including our schools. What is fascinating to me is that some of the very institutions, businesses, and industries for which we have traditionally prepared our students are the ones that are leading the way in reconstructing our notions of schools and education. What is even more interesting is that they are reclaiming our turf as their own, and they are actively using some of the strategies school systems talk about as being best practice, but which schools rarely implement. These innovative organizations have been thoughtful, strategic, creative, and bold in their thinking, and therefore have created models for the future of education.

For instance, Microsoft's "School of the Future" concept is based on five critical factors that shape their focus (www.microsoft.com):

1. An involved and connected learning community

2. A proficient and inviting curriculum-driven community

3. A flexible and sustainable learning environment

4. A cross-curriculum integration of research and development

5. Professional leadership

This has since evolved into the Innovative Schools Program, which has become a worldwide initiative of Microsoft to create a network of schools committed to "working collaboratively, using research-based learning principles and best-in-class technology, integrated and adapted for local community needs" (www.microsoft.com/education/pil/).

In Apple's "Classroom of Tomorrow—Today" (ACOT^2) program, there are six design principles that form the basis of their collaborative partnership with the educational community to provide a vision for 21st-century high schools:

1. Understanding of 21st-century skills and outcomes

2. Relevant and applied curriculum

3. Informative assessment

4. A culture of innovation and creativity

5. Social and emotional connections with students

6. Ubiquitous access to technology

HASTAC (Humanities, Arts, Science, and Technology Advanced Collaboratory), a virtual, collaborative group of scholars around the world from the disciplines mentioned in the group's name, is committed to three principles fundamental to the future of learning: "first, the creative use and development of new technologies for learning and research; second, critical understanding of the role of new media in life, learning, and society; and third, pedagogical advancement of the goals of participatory learning" (Davidson and Goldberg, 2009).

The Knowledge Works foundation, whose central focus is on high school reform, has drafted ten principles they contend are the basis for the work of schools (www.futureofed.org):

1. Self-learning

2. Horizontal structures

3. Moving from presumed authority to collective credibility

4. A decentered pedagogy

5. Networked learning

6. Open-sourced education

7. Learning as connectivity and interactivity

8. Lifelong learning

9. Learning institutions as mobilizing networks

10. Flexible scalability and simulation

Tony Wagner (2008) from Harvard University suggests that in 21st-century schools, there are seven survival skills students need to be taught:

1. Critical thinking and problem solving

2. Collaboration across networks and leading by influence

3. Agility and adaptability

4. Initiative and entrepreneurialism

5. Effective oral and written communication

6. Accessing and analyzing information

7. Curiosity and imagination

In the same book, Wagner makes reference to the work of Litkey and Washor, who created MET (The Metropolitan Regional Career and Technical Center) schools, first in Rhode Island, and now also in New York state. They propose five learning goals for schools:

1. Communication

2. Empirical learning

3. Personal qualities

4. Quantitative reasoning

5. Social reasoning

The Oracle Foundation, originators of the ThinkQuest global competition, likewise operate from a vision of what the future of schooling should be like. Their leadership in reinventing schools and education is pinned to the following values and beliefs: "[Our] mission is to inspire students globally to think, connect, create and share—using technology to help them dissolve boundaries, fulfill their potential, and create a better society" (www.oraclefoundation.org).

ThinkQuest is designed to advance student engagement through new, exciting modes of learning. Students around the world are able to "compete" collaboratively on solving a global issue, the premise behind the powerful learning strategy of problem-based learning. Trilling and Fadel (2009) describe a recent project entry in this global challenge: "The six student team members, working from four different time zones, exchanged nearly 3,000 messages in the course of their project. They used over a dozen different software and Web tools to create and share their work online, constantly adding, editing, and modifying one another's work as they developed their Web site."

In their book *21st Century Skills: Learning for Life in Our Times,* Trilling and Fadel suggest that the work of schools in the future should be shaped by five considerations: authentic learning, mental model building, internal motivation, multiple intelligences, and social learning.

Napa Valley, California's High Tech High, a charter school developed and nurtured by its originator and intellectual godfather Larry Rosenstock, was conceived when a group of about 40 high-tech leaders and civic leaders came together in the late 1990s and put together their version of a school for the future, driven by the growing lack of competent human resources for the tech industry of the day. Larry Rosenstock was hired to become the founding principal of the charter school, which opened its doors in September 2000. Today, there is an integrated network of such schools in the area that continues to grow at a time when other schools systems are struggling under the weight of budget cuts and diminished resources. This vision was shaped by the specific design principles of personalization, real-world connections, and a common intellectual mission (www.hightechhigh.org).

In every instance, these "schools of the future" began their dream by creating a vision of a preferred future. From them, we need to learn, first, that a school of the future is possible, and second that it can't just be a variation of our current ineffective models. Times have changed drastically, and exceptional problems will surely require exceptional solutions.

We need to pursue a more hopeful vision—a vision of possibility, rather than a painful review of past and current challenges. We need to be mindful of the past, but not handcuffed by it. We need to respect the past, but not be afraid to distance ourselves from it. We need to embrace the past, because it has shaped the foundation for our new future. We need to use the stories or lessons from the past to avoid making mistakes in the future. We will surely make mistakes, but if we heed the lessons of the past, they will not be the same ones.

There are several areas we must explore to form the basis for the school of the future. First, we must create the foundation for future learning. What have we learned about learning that will be essential in our new school? Second, there are some ethical challenges that must be addressed in order to move ahead with this work. Third, we must figure out what facilities might house our school of the future. Last, we must create a vision of the school of the future. These are not the only issues that need to be addressed. We must all raise questions, ponder possibilities, and share our thoughts on 21st-century education. After all, none of us alone has all the answers. It is the power of a collaborative environment that will lead to the profundity of creative thought that can make these ideas come alive.

As Davidson and Goldberg (2009) explain, "If we are going to imagine new learning institutions that are not based on the contiguity of time and place—*virtual* institutions—we have to ask, what are those institutions and what work do they perform? What does a virtual learning institution look like, who supports it, what does it do? We know that informal learning happens, constantly and in many new ways, because of the collaborative opportunities offered by social networking sites, wikis, blogs, and many other interactive digital sources."

We must base our vision of the school of the future on those questions, and on those realities.

A NEW VISION

We need to identify our vision for the school of the future. There are many things to consider, including the role of the student, the nature of learning, and approaches to get the students on the path to lifelong learning and to see that they are intrinsically motivated to pursue their passions. We must consider the value of collaborative opportunities using the power of technologies that make learning and teaching anywhere, anytime, and anyhow possible.

Our vision of teaching and learning is built on problem-based inquiry, an approach that begins with the statement of a real-world issue. Students then provide thoughtful consideration that leads to a real action plan to deal with that issue or concern. Implicit in this form of learning is the need to identify the big ideas and essential questions of the issue. Coupled with this is the expectation that there should be a culminating project to benefit the community that students would be expected to defend to a jury of their peers and community leaders.

Our school would incorporate some of the ideas proposed by Christensen (2008), ideas such as customized or personalized learning, student-centric classrooms, and the deployment of computers to all students.

Ideally, this would not necessitate an actual school to which the students would travel each day, but that may be too far to reach at the outset, so we would examine our present schools to see what adaptations could be made to create some of this "disruptive innovation" (Christensen, 2008).

First, we need to consider how schools are currently organized. Traditional learning paradigms tend to be passive, insulated, prescribed, and hierarchal (www.plearn.net). I have yet to encounter a school that does not have someone named as the principal or head of the school, whose responsibility it is to lead the school in all aspects of the school's function. This individual usually has the authority to hire teachers, organize the students' and teachers' schedules, manage the financial resources of the school, and encourage parents to participate in some type of parent-teacher council to whom the principal must occasionally report on a myriad of subjects. This may be a simplistic depiction of the role of the principal, but it is clearly an old top-down model of organization that pervades the present school organizational system. Some principals seem very effective, while others, doing the same job, struggle. So, while there is evidence that school leadership is important to the success of the school, leadership is second to the significance of classroom instruction (Hattie, 2009).

Does it not make sense, then, to consider other means of school leadership that more directly reflect collaborative approaches? Do we need principals to run schools at all? Could collaborative teams of teachers and other school-based personnel manage all the duties and functions presently assigned to the principal of a school? Teachers would say that it is not their job to run the school, and there might be some justification for that claim. However, think of some of the issues that might be resolved if teams of teachers ran their own affairs. Unions, as we presently know them, would not be necessary under such a system, because they exist to make sure teachers are protected from over-assignment, unreasonable salaries, and unfair dismissal by someone (the principal or school board) in a position of higher authority.

Social networks, advanced greatly by the use of technology, are a model for our schools to emulate. Teachers working collaboratively could function admirably to organize, run, and monitor all aspects of the school with less turmoil than they currently experience. The involvement of students would also be welcome. There are few examples where students are given an active voice or input into the day-to-day organization and running of the school, even though they represent the greatest proportion of the participants in that institution. Student councils do not constitute the type of participation I speak of. I am not talking about clubs or occasional consultation, but rather real participatory involvement in the organization and running of the school.

In England, there was a "The School I'd Like" competition in which students were encouraged to submit a design of their own school (Burke and Grosvenor, 2003). The competition "unleashed the most imaginative, stimulating and provocative challenges to our educational system. And those challenges have come entirely from children. Entrusted with designing their own schools, where they spend an average working week, they have grasped the opportunity. They want change" (www.guardian.co.uk/education). What the students wanted, as described in "The Children's Manifesto" was (Burke and Grosvenor, 2003):

> a beautiful school
> a comfortable school
> a safe school
> a listening school
> a flexible school
> a relevant school
> a respectful school
> a school without walls
> a school for everybody.

We need to think carefully about how schools first came to be, sort of a "back to the future" concept. For schools to be viable in the future, we need to reformulate a partnership with the organizations that gave rise to schools in the first place; industry, businesses, and community organizations should become active leaders in creating our new schools. Consider how useful and productive it would be to have local business and industry sponsor the schools in their respective communities. Those businesses could support financially the growth and development of the schools of the future. Profits could be put into creating self-sustaining schools that would then not be prone to the vagaries of budget shortfalls they are presently plagued by. Collaborative partnerships with business, industry, and local communities would create a circle of responsibility for schools beyond the small group that currently bears the brunt of the litany of complaints when schools are not performing up to standard on the world stage.

It has been said repeatedly that schools have to prepare students for the "real world." That world is usually described in terms of jobs. As Trilling and Fadel (2009) write, "In short, pressure is increasing on education systems around the world to teach in ways that will produce the knowledge, workers, and innovators businesses need to be successful in the 21st century and the knowledge economy."

It makes sense for the businesses and industries that will benefit directly from the students who will graduate from our future schools to participate intimately in helping to design, finance, support, and lead the development of a new model of schooling.

Davidson and Goldberg (2009) describe what it will take to create learning institutions that will embrace the technologies industry will surely demand:

> This book proposes a deliberately provocative alternative definition of institution: An institution as a mobilizing network. This counterintuitive (and even cantankerous) definition is a way to rethink the limits of an institution and its potential. Given that the aim is to consider learning institutions for a digital age, what might follow from a definition of institution that emphasized its flexibility, the permeability of its boundaries, its interactive productivity, and its potential as a catalyst for change rather than its mechanisms of cooperation, order, control, and regulation?

These new institutions must also be mindful of current policies designed to regulate the behavior and comportment of the students with regard to technology. Currently, most schools have policies regarding the use of cell phones, and procedures for the use of school computers. Many of these rules contravene teachers' wishes to use these devices for instructional purposes. Many teachers have learned to use the cell phone as an instructional tool, much like the calculator. But schools invariably have regulations against the use of cell phones by students. There are ethical issues that need to be considered regarding the flood of information that cell phones and computers provide access to, and controversies will inevitably follow the acceptance of such technology.

Recall the battle that still rages over what novels and other reading material are appropriate for inclusion in school libraries.

In British Columbia, Canada, in 2011, parents are waging all-out war against a school district that has authorized wireless technology for the students. Parents claim that many of their children are becoming sick since the implementation of this technology. What impact will that have on schools' ability to provide their children with the tools needed for this new age of education and schooling?

That is just the tip of the ethical iceberg: confidentiality, respect of individual rights, missing files, hackers, online bullying, and other yet-to-be-seen problems must be considered. Parents currently struggle to control the use of these devices in their own homes. Schools, with larger groups and challenging circumstances, have even greater obstacles to overcome in managing their use. There may well be no easy answers, but we cannot neglect to address these issues if we ever hope to achieve our dream of technologically integrated schools.

It has always been the case that educators must, as the song from *The Man from La Mancha* suggests, "dream the impossible dream" and "no matter how hopeless," must "reach the unreachable star."

But now, that star is no longer unreachable. We have within our grasp opportunities and challenges that could take us to places in the world of education we have never even imagined. What will it take for you to join the adventure, or better still, lead the revolution?

Conclusion

I T WAS THE BEST OF TIMES, it was the worst of times." Charles Dickens' opening line in his classic *A Tale of Two Cities* is probably one of the most quoted phrases of all time, since it so aptly summarizes the eternal tension between crisis and opportunity. And it can very well apply to education in the 21st century.

Yes, it may be the worst of times. We are a generation of educators caught up in the maelstrom of a violent transition, finding ourselves woefully unequipped to deal with a completely new and changed knowledge paradigm. The teaching profession's collective self-esteem is bordering on an all-time low, there is an evident lack of a clear vision to navigate change, and society is confused and uncertain about what to expect from schools. More and more is demanded from educators, there is mounting pressure from governmental agencies that supervise education all over the world, budgets are being slashed in public education everywhere, and, at least in the United States, statistics regarding dropouts, graduation rates, and the level of engagement of students are quite unflattering.

But I tend to think that it is, really, the best of times.

For several years prior to becoming a school administrator and thus switching from a full-time to a full-life job, I worked developing educational projects for the space program, and during those very enjoyable years I not only learned a great deal about space exploration, but also came across many inspirational stories from the men and women who selflessly dedicated their lives to the cause of exploring space.

I am fond of telling a story from Gene Kranz, the Apollo lead flight director whom I mentioned in a previous chapter as having coined the famous phrase "Failure is not an option." In the midst of the Apollo 13 crisis, when things were falling apart, both literally on the spacecraft and at Mission Control, where the team was having difficulty finding solutions to the life-threatening problems the crew were facing, Gene Kranz was confronted by Chris Kraft, his mentor, who pessimistically said of the impending loss of life of the three astronauts in deep space: "This could be the worst disaster that NASA has ever faced." Gene Kranz squared up and replied, "With all due respect, sir, I believe this could be our finest hour."

OUR FINEST HOUR

I also believe that this could be our finest hour. This educational crisis of unfathomable proportions, and the changes that are seemingly leaving us baffled, also provide a wonderful opportunity to create a better educational system. We are the first generation of learners to have access to all accumulated human knowledge. Advances in communications allow us to cooperate like never before, to augment our individual capacity in ways that were hitherto unknown. There is an increased awareness of others, of inequalities, and of the problems that we face on Earth regarding overpopulation and pollution, and the extensive development of social networks allows us to truly become a global community that can attempt to live in tolerance and peace.

It is the best time in history to be an educator, because it is within our power to educate the generation that can make use of these gifts to turn the knowledge era into an era of true enlightenment.

EDUCATION'S MOON SHOT

This whole book is about harnessing powerful ideas and drivers, and finding the motivation to jump-start change. I have acknowledged many times that implementation is a much more difficult road than imagination, and one that, unfortunately, is plagued with external constraints. Schools are conservative businesses, and are used to step-by-step incremental processes.

However, and despite understanding the need for caution, I want to conclude with a call to develop a bold vision and act upon it. To borrow once more from the space program, not everybody knows that the real vision for space exploration was to go to Mars, and that the moon shot was regarded as an intermediate step in the process. It turned out that the moon shot was the wrong intermediate step towards getting to Mars, but nobody at the time could have foretold that 40 years after the moon landing, humans would not be an inch closer to Mars than they were at the time, and that even replicating that feat would be impossible today.

In 21st-century education, we need to target our moon shots very carefully, lest we, for the sake of not disrupting the status quo, choose the wrong intermediate steps. We have only one chance to capture the public's imagination about a completely new educational system that will deliver on the promise of a better education for all. Paradoxically, going about change in slow incremental steps may be more risky than trying to materialize a daring vision. It is not just our duty, but our moral imperative to do all in our power to act on what we know, for the benefit of our students.

Martin Luther King once said, "Our lives begin to end the day we become silent about the things that matter." Transforming an educational system that is not serving well the students under our charge is something that really matters. Let our lives as educators begin again, and not begin to end.

References

Abbott, A. (2007, April). Mozart doesn't make you clever. www.nature.com/news/2007/070413/full/news070409-13.html

Bennett, B. (2010). *Graphic intelligence: Playing with possibilities.* Ajax, Ontario: Bookation.

Bennett, B., & Rolheiser, C. (2001). *Beyond Monet: The artful science of instructional integration.* Toronto, Ontario: Bookation.

Bonk, C. J. (2009) *The world is open: How Web technology is revolutionizing education.* San Francisco, CA: Jossey-Bass.

Burke, C., & Grosvenor, I. (2003). *The school I'd like: Children and young people's reflections on an education for the 21st century.* London: RoutledgeFalmer.

Carr, N. (2011). *The shallows: What the internet is doing to our brains.* New York: W. W. Norton & Company.

Chen, M. (2010). *Education nation: Six leading edges of innovation in our schools.* San Francisco, CA: Jossey-Bass.

Christensen, C. M. (2008). *Disrupting class: How disruptive innovation will change the way the world learns.* New York: McGraw-Hill.

Collins, J. (2001). *Good to great: Why some companies make the leap . . . and others don't.* New York: HarperCollins.

Cross, J. (2006). *Informal learning: Rediscovering the natural pathways that inspire innovation and performance.* San Francisco, CA: Pfeiffer.

Cuban, L. (1993). Computers meet classroom: Classroom wins. *Teachers College Record, 95*(2), 185–210.

Cuban, L. (2005). *The blackboard and the bottom line: Why schools can't be businesses.* Cambridge, MA: Harvard University Press.

Darling-Hammond, L. (2010). *The flat world and education: How America's commitment to equity will determine our future.* New York: Teachers College Press.

Darling-Hammond, L., et al. (2008). *Powerful learning: What we know about teaching for understanding.* San Francisco, CA: Jossey-Bass.

Davidson, C. N., & Goldberg, D. T. (2009). *The future of learning institutions in a digital age.* (John D. and Catherine T. MacArthur Foundation Reports on Digital Media and Learning). Cambridge, MA: MIT Press.

195

Dean, C. (2008, July 22). If you have a problem, ask everyone. *New York Times.* www.nytimes.com

De Saint-Exupéry, A. (1943). *The little prince.*

Dweck, C. S. (2006). *Mindset: The new psychology of success.* New York: Random House.

Elmore, R. (2006, July). Presentation at Harvard Institute for School Leadership, Cambridge, MA.

Friedman, T. (2005). *The world is flat: A brief history of the twenty-first century.* New York: Farrar, Straus and Giroux.

Friedman, T. (2007). *The world is flat 3.0: A brief history of the twenty-first century* (expanded edition). New York: Farrar, Straus and Giroux.

Gardner, H. (1983). *Frames of mind: The theory of multiple intelligences.* New York: Basic Books.

Gardner, H. (2006). *Multiple intelligences: New horizons in theory and practice.* New York: Basic Books.

Gardner, H. (2009). *Five minds for the future.* Boston, MA: Harvard Business School Press.

Guskey, T. (2007). *The principal as assessment leader.* ESSARP Conference, San Miguel del Monte, Argentina.

Hargreaves, A. (2010). Leadership, change and beyond the 21st century skills agenda. In J. Bellanca & R. Brandt (Eds.), *21st century skills: Rethinking how students learn.* (Leading Edge series). Bloomington, IN: Solution Tree.

Hargreaves, A., & Shirley, D. L. (Eds). (2009). *The fourth way: The inspiring future for educational change.* Thousand Oaks, CA: Corwin Press.

Hattie, J. (2009). *Visible learning: A synthesis of over 800 meta-analyses relating to achievement.* New York: Routledge.

Heifetz, R. (2006, July). Challenges of leadership. Harvard Institute for School Improvement, Harvard University.

Heifetz, R., & Linsky, M. (2002). *Leadership on the line: Staying alive through the dangers of leading.* Boston, MA: Harvard Business Press.

Jacobs, H. H. (2010). *Curriculum 21: Essential education for a changing world.* Alexandria, VA: ASCD.

Killion, J., & Roy, P. (2009). *Becoming a learning school.* Ohio: National Staff Development Council.

Kurtzman, J., & Goldsmith, M. (2010). *Common purpose: How great leaders get organizations to achieve the extraordinary.* San Francisco, CA: Jossey-Bass.

Kurzweil, R. (2005). *The singularity is near: When humans transcend biology.* London: Penguin.

Lawrence, T. E. (1926). *The seven pillars of wisdom.*

Liu, E., & Noppe-Brandon, S. (2009). *Imagination first: Unlocking the power of possibility.* San Francisco, CA: Jossey-Bass.

Marzano, R. (2007). *The art and science of teaching: A comprehensive framework for effective instruction.* Alexandria, VA: Association for Supervision and Curriculum Development.

Marzano, R. (Ed). (2010). *On excellence in teaching.* Bloomington, IN: Solution Tree.

McPherson, T. (Ed). (2007). A pedagogy for original synners. In *Digital youth, innovation, and the unexpected.* Cambridge, MA: MIT Press.

Nair, P., Fielding, R., & Lackney, J. (2005). *The language of school design: Design patterns for 21st century schools.* Minneapolis, MN: DesignShare.

National Research Council. (2001). *Knowing what students know: The science of design and educational assessment.* Washington, DC: National Academy Press.

OECD/CERI International Conference. (2008). *Learning in the 21st century: Research, innovation and policy.* Assessment for Learning Formative Assessment. Paris, France.

OWP/P Architecture, VS Furniture, and Bruce Mau Design. (2010). *The third teacher: 79 ways you can use design to transform teaching and learning.* New York: Abrams.

Palmer, P. (1999). *Let your life speak.* San Francisco, CA: Jossey-Bass.

Palmer, P. (2007). *The courage to teach: Exploring the inner landscape of a teacher's life.* San Francisco, CA: Jossey-Bass.

Pearlman, B. (2010). Designing new learning environments to support 21st century skills. In J. Bellanca & R. Brandt (Eds.), *21st century skills: Rethinking how students learn.* (Leading Edge series). Bloomington, IN: Solution Tree.

Piaget, J. (1998). *Origins of intelligence in children.* New York: W. W. Norton.

Pink, D. H. (2006). *A whole new mind: Why right-brainers will rule the future.* New York: Riverhead.

Pink, D. H. (2009). *Drive: The surprising truth about what motivates us.* New York: Riverhead.

Prensky, M. (2001, October). Digital natives, digital immigrants. *On the Horizon, 9*(5).

Reeves, D. B. (2006). *The learning leader: How to focus school improvement for better results.* Alexandria, VA: ASCD.

Reeves, D. B. (2007a). *The daily disciplines of leadership: How to improve student achievement, staff motivation, and personal organization.* San Francisco, CA: Jossey-Bass.

Reeves, D. B. (2007b). *Closing the implementation gap.* ESSARP Conference, Rosario, Argentina.

Riley, K. (2008). Can schools successfully meet their educational aims without the clear support of their local communities? *Journal of Educational Change, 9*(3).

Robinson, K. (2001). *Out of our minds: Learning to be creative.* West Sussex, UK: Capstone.

Robinson, K. (2006). *Ken Robinson Says Schools Kill Creativity.* TED Talks. www.ted.com/talks/lang/eng/ken_robinson_says_schools_kill_creativity.html

Robinson, K., & Aronica, L. (2009). *The element: How finding your passion changes everything.* London: Penguin.

Rose, A. (2010). Keynote address. ESSARP Conference, San Miguel del Monte, Argentina.

Saphier, J., & Gower, R. (1997). *The skillful teacher: Building our teaching skills.* Acton, MS: Research for Better Teaching.

Schwartz, B. (2009, February). *The loss of wisdom.* TED conference, Long Beach, CA.

Sinek, S. (2009). *Start with why: How great leaders inspire everyone to take action.* London: Portfolio.

Sternberg, R. J. (1988). *The triarchic mind: A new theory of human intelligence.* New York: Viking Adult.

Thornburg, D. (1997). *Campfires in cyberspace: Primordial metaphors for learning in the 21st century.* www.tcpd.org/thornburg/handouts/campfires.pdf

Tomlinson, C. A., & McTighe, J. (2006). *Integrating differentiated instruction + understanding by design: Connecting content and kids.* Alexandria, VA: Association for Supervision and Curriculum Development.

Trilling, B., & Fadel, C. (2009). *21st century skills: Learning for life in our times.* San Francisco, CA: Jossey-Bass.

Tufte, E. (1997). *Visual explanations: Images and quantities, evidence and narrative.* Connecticut: Graphics Press.

UK Department for Education. (2004). *A national conversation about personalised learning.*

Vollmer, J. (2010). *Schools cannot do it alone: Building public support for America's public schools.* Santa Clara, CA: Enlightenment Press.

Vygotsky, L. (1962). *Thought and language.* Cambridge, MA: MIT Press.

Wagner, T. (2008). *The global achievement gap: Why even our best schools don't teach the new survival skills our children need—and what to do about it.* New York: Basic Books.

Wallis, C. (2006, Dec. 10). How to bring our schools out of the 20th century. *Time.* www.timemagazine.com

Wiliam, D. (2008). *Classroom assessment: Minute by minute and day by day.* ASCD Annual Conference, New Orleans.

Zhao, Y. (2009). *Catching up or leading the way: American education in the age of globalization.* Alexandria, VA: ASCD.

Web sites

Sites with no specific access date listed are current as of March 15, 2011.

www.21stcenturythinker.com/2010/05/drilling-for-cognition-building-without.html. May 26, 2010.

www.bcse.uk.net/downloads//69A_Learning_Journey.pdf. *Learning journeys: Moving towards designs for new learning places: Two truths and a suggestion.*

www.crito.uci.edu/tlc/findings/co-nect/startpage.html. May 23, 2010.

www.designshare.com

www.earthsky.org/health/earl-miller-says-younger-generation-will-be -better-multitaskers. March 24, 2011.

www.education.qld.gov.au/corporate/newbasics/html/richtasks/richtasks .html

www.education.washington.edu/areas/tep/. May 26, 2010.

www.edutopia.org/it-takes-village-and-museum

www.elschools.org. May 23, 2010.

www.en.wikipedia.org/wiki/Lev_Vygotsky. March 23, 2011.

www.fora.tv/2009/08/14/George_Kembel_Awakening_Creativity

www.fridayreflections.typepad.com/weblog/2007/09/but-weve-always.html

www.futureofed.org. Nov. 10, 2010.

www.guardian.co.uk/education/2001/jun/05/schools.uk7. March 23, 2011.

www.hansonrobotics.wordpress.com

www.hightechhigh.org/about/. Dec. 18, 2010.

www.hightechhigh.org/unboxed/issue1/why_we_did_it/. Dec. 18, 2010.

www.ipsos-na.com/news-polls/pressrelease.aspx?id=4957

www.jason.org/public/whatis/start.aspx. May 23, 2010.

www.knowledgeworks.org/vision/our-beliefs/how-we-create-change.
    Dec. 18, 2010.

www.management-issues.com/2006/5/24/mentors/jim-collins-and-level-5
    -leadership.asp

www.metiri.com

www.microsoft.com/education/pil/ISc_ProgramOverview.aspx

www.microsoft.com/education/schoolofthefuture/. Nov. 20, 2010.

www.nature.com/news/2010/100420/full/464111a.html. March 23, 2011.

www.nimh.nih.gov/health/publications/teenage-brain-a-work-in-progress
    -fact-sheet/index.shtml. March 24, 2011.

www.oecd.org. March 23, 2010.

www.oraclefoundation.org. March 23, 2011.

www.plearn.net. Dec. 20, 2010.

www.stanford.edu/dept/SUSE/cgi-bin/ldt/about/index.html. May 26, 2010.

www.technovelgy.com/ct/Science-Fiction-News.asp?NewsNum=2805. See
    Korean Robot Teaching Assistants.

www.ted.com/talks/lang/eng/dan_pink_on_motivation.html. March 15,
    2011.

www.ted.com/talks/lang/eng/sugata_mitra_shows_how_kids_teach_
    themselves.html. Nov. 20, 2010.

www.theblueschool.org. May 26, 2010.

www.usfirst.org/aboutus/content.aspx?id=34. May 26, 2010.

www.usgbc.org/LEED

Index